T0156419

Finding YOUR Joy

MARGARET T. COLEMAN

WESTBOW®
PRESS
A DIVISION OF THOMAS NELSON
& ZONDERVAN

First Edition.

Scripture quotations are taken from the Holy Bible, King James Version.

Author Credits: "Margaret's writing is inspirational and encouraging with many incidences which could take place in our own lives…"

WestBow Press books may be ordered through booksellers or by contacting:

WestBow Press
A Division of Thomas Nelson & Zondervan
1663 Liberty Drive
Bloomington, IN 47403
www.westbowpress.com
1 (866) 928-1240

ISBN: 978-1-4908-3969-1 (sc)
ISBN: 978-1-4908-3970-7 (hc)
ISBN: 978-1-4908-3971-4 (e)

Library of Congress Control Number: 2014910265

Printed in the United States of America.

WestBow Press rev. date: 6/19/2014

Contents

To my mother, Mrs. Cynthia Bryant-Tate: thank you for your quiet, patient love. You were always there for me. I thank God he chose you to be my mom and best friend.

Children are a blessing and a special gift. Doyle and I are thankful for our special gifts, David and Deborah.

Joy is prayer. Joy is strength. Joy is love. Joy is
a net of love by which you can catch souls.
—Mother Teresa (1910–1997)

I will sing to the Lord as long as I live. I
will praise God to my last breath! May
he be pleased by all these thoughts about
him, for *he is the source of all my joy.*
—Psalm 105:33–34 (emphasis added)

Acknowledgments

First and foremost, I would like to thank God for the insight and opportunity to share what he has revealed to me. For we know that all good and perfect gifts come from God.

Thanks to Doyle, my husband, and Deborah, my daughter, for encouraging my endeavor—and especially to Deborah for helping me stay on track and encouraging me to finish my project.

Thanks to my sisters, Ruby and Cynthia, who got me started writing my ABCs and reading simple books before I started kindergarten, which gave me my foundation and love for reading.

A special thanks to all those contributors who were gracious enough to share their personal joy, which adds life to this concept.

Thanks to Gloria Sydnor, Sophia Sattar, and Fran Mullen for assisting me in organizing my thoughts. I couldn't have done this without you. To everyone who helped with editing and printing—and most of all, to my faithful readers: I truly thank you from the bottom of my heart.

Please enjoy!

1

My Story

Margaret T. Coleman
Author, Personal Financial Advisor

Joy in Springtime

It was a beautiful spring day, and the air was fresh and clean—a good time to roll down the windows and feel the warm breeze. What a wonderful time of year! We feel free, released from our heavy winter attire. We can relax and stand tall without the need to buffer ourselves against the cold winds of winter.

Spring has arrived, and telltale signs are everywhere. If only we could bottle this feeling of anticipation! Previously, we had no desire to be outdoors, but now we are making plans that include activities beyond the confines of our winter haven. There are indications that something new and exciting is about to happen.

Each day we are awakened by the lovely sound of chirping birds as they return from warmer winter retreats. Some birds fly thousands of miles during the migration season. By instinct alone, they feel the change in the air and begin their annual trip north, once again following the age-old ritual of mating, building nests, and raising their offspring.

Driving along the road, we can see neighbors raking dead leaves and removing fallen tree limbs and all remnants of winter from their lawns. Some are seeding their lawns, expecting beautiful, plush, green grass to eventually appear. Others are repairing fences, shutters, and mailboxes and giving them a much-needed coat of paint.

It is quite a sight to behold the miracle of nature's transformation from barren to beautiful, the various trees and bushes all producing their individual colored buds.

Thinking about why trees and bushes have many different colored buds before the green leaves and beautiful flowers appear, we conclude that it's God's way of adding color to the bland scene we've witnessed during the long winter months.

One of the most beautiful sights of spring can be seen in Washington, DC, when the beautiful cherry blossoms appear. A cherry blossom is the flower of a cherry tree, which is also known as *sakura*.

Each year the National Cherry Blossom Festival begins in late March and runs through mid-April. The festival is held as a reminder of the gift of over three thousand cherry trees from the mayor of Tokyo to Washington in 1912. More than a million people travel to the nation's capital to observe the thousands of cherry trees and to participate in the festival's activities.

The main attraction is at the Tidal Basin, where thousands of pink and white flowers bloom alongside monuments to Thomas Jefferson, George Washington, Abraham Lincoln, and Dr. Martin Luther King Jr. Can you imagine your own purpose and joy producing a life that's honored and remembered in such a way?

We are like the dormant trees, plants, and bushes that come alive again in springtime. Within us is the ability to produce a budding *joy* that will come to life if properly fed, cultivated, and nurtured. We too can transform and make a tremendous difference by adding beauty and enjoyment to life out of our God-given joy. Our purpose and joy are intentionally entwined.

Imagine that our lives are like a cherry tree that has many purposes:

1. The trees have *beautiful buds* that are pleasant to behold. Our display of *Christ within us* can make us pleasant to behold.
2. The *leaves* provide shade from the midday sun. Our lives can provide *hope and encouragement* to the discouraged.
3. The tree can be a *nesting place* for birds. Our hearts can be a nesting place and source of *outpouring love*.
4. Some trees provide cherries for *nourishment*. We can provide *spiritual food* for nourishment.

What a beautiful contribution!

Personal Joy

Finding our real joy might take some time, but it's worth looking for, digging deep within and searching for what gives the utmost pleasure. It's a treasure worth finding, and it's personal.

We can't put a price on it, but we can benefit greatly from it. We have freedom to express ourselves in our own way, doing what pleases us most. We don't need to be afraid to be ourselves.

Simply stated, we need to find our joy to make life complete.

We want to use our allotted time to the fullest, and we only have one chance to leave our footprints in the sands of time. When we look back, we want to be able to say that we've done everything we could to contribute, that we've enjoyed every minute, and that we are thankful for our journey.

The Scripture states: "Trust in the Lord with all your heart, and lean not on your own understanding. In all your ways acknowledge him, and He shall direct your paths" (Proverbs 3:5–6). Our joy and our direction in all things come from the Lord.

The world has set standards that can cause much frustration if we try to live up to them. Such standards take our focus off our own self-worth and cause us to gaze at the accomplishments of others. In our minds, we exaggerate acts that receive public notice, and we desire to be in that same position of perceived importance. Don't forget the big picture: we *all* count and are very important in life's big scheme. But coming to this conclusion isn't easy. Others' achievements may cloud our view.

Consider a sold-out sporting event with prime-time coverage on the number-one TV network. Newspaper reporters, sports writers, commentators, cameramen, statisticians, ticket agents, ushers, souvenir vendors, and all the stadium employees have arrived.

The managers, trainers, umpires, and players are right on time. The two best rival teams are the center of attention. The most dedicated and gifted star players are about to perform, and they assure us they deserve all the praise and accolades they receive.

Excitement is in the air. A crowd of more than thirty thousand fans begins to arrive, hours before game time, to cheer for their favorite team. With cameras and binoculars in hand, they hope to catch a close-up memento that will last a lifetime. Tailgaters are equipped with barbecue pits, their favorite food, chairs, and games—and all-weather gear, just in case. They are looking forward to hot dogs, peanuts, and Cracker Jacks as they witness one of America's favorite games. The description alone brings back pleasant memories.

All the *important* people have arrived, but there is one small problem. The person we think about the least—the *unimportant* person who has the key that allows everyone access to the stadium—is nowhere to be found. What an important job he has! And yet I wonder if anyone even knows his name?

In order for this day to be successful, everyone mentioned must be present—especially the person who affords everyone access to the day's action. He has a job that receives little fanfare or notoriety, but he is the superstar of the day.

Whatever your role in life, large or small, you are a very important and necessary part of the "big picture."

I witnessed this scenario when I went to Shea Stadium in New York to see the highly publicized subway series between the New York Mets and the New York Yankees. We rode in a chartered bus, enjoying nice weather and friendly interchange among passengers.

I had the opportunity to see, in person, the superstars I'd seen on television, such as Derrick Jeter, Alex Rodriquez, Jose Reyes, and David Wright, to mention a few. The most enjoyable part of the day was the moment when the Mets won. There's nothing like being at the stadium to watch a game, but you have to be attentive. There are no commentators giving you the play-by-play, and you have to watch the scoreboard, the field, and the large screen for stats—and for the prompts to make noise and root, root, root for your team.

It was an enjoyable, fun-filled day—an experience I wouldn't have had if the man with the key hadn't arrived.

Individuals

All of us have our own unique DNA and fingerprints. God set us apart to be individuals, and there are no carbon copies. He has supplied all the ingredients that make us special. He has deposited everything we need into our lives so we can make withdrawals and live a fulfilled life.

Isn't it amazing that, out of all the millions and billions of babies born, God put his special stamp on each of us? We are special, different, compact, and complete. God created heaven and earth, the moon and stars, and he has carefully and intentionally crafted us as individuals.

The color of our eyes and hair, our height, talents, abilities, emotions, and *joy* are all preplanned and given to us by God alone. We have no input or influence.

God gives all of us something that gives us extreme joy.

What is joy? According to *Webster's Dictionary, joy* is:

- A lively emotion of happiness, delight, and pleasure
- Anything causing such emotion
- The expression of such emotions
- Being glad, rejoicing
- Cheerfulness, glee, happiness, and merriment

That's how we want to live.

After the shades have been raised and the curtains have been drawn back so that the light shines in on our own personal and private joy, then we can indulge in delight over our lives. Our skills and talents are not intended to make us puffed up or arrogant. They are gifts, and we should feel humble gratitude that we have been favored to achieve in our various fields.

My Beginnings

I'm told that my arrival was on a cold, sunny Sunday in February. My parents probably wondered what the future would hold for me, what my destiny would be.

I was the baby of the family and a mama's girl. My mother's love was quiet and peaceful. We always got along and had a special relationship.

Some of my earliest memories of her are from my preschool days. She fixed my breakfast, which I had to finish before going out to play. Sometimes it took hours, but she patiently went about her business until I finished.

I still have vivid memories of following her around, listening to her talk and tell me stories. When she cooked, I imitated her actions with my own play kitchen set. When she baked a cake, she always gave me a small portion of batter to taste. She was a good cook, and her food was delicious, so I sacrificed my own pretend meals to eat hers.

When my mother's friends came by for their woman-to-woman chats, they allowed me to stay and play in the same room—if I was quiet. But if I asked questions or got into their conversation, I had to go play in another room. Naturally I learned to be quiet and enjoyed the good fellowship they had. My mother was always there for me: when I graduated, got married, and had my children, and even when I had the opportunity to retire early.

When I was four, my two older sisters, Ruby and Cynthia, were preparing for the new school year. I joined in the excitement but was disappointed to learn that I had to wait until the following year to start my formal educational journey. To make me feel better, my mom asked my sisters to set up a schoolroom atmosphere for me. I had a blackboard with chalk and eraser, crayons, coloring book, paper, and pencils. I also had assignments to complete each day.

Those assignments were easy, so they began to challenge me with first grade material, which I also completed. I had to write, draw, color within the lines, and do math problems, all of which they checked for accuracy and neatness. As time when by, the little *Dick and Jane* books became my favorites. I loved the dog named Spot. "See Spot run. Run, Spot, run." I read those little books over and over.

Those activities laid the foundation for what I still enjoy today: reading. In my makeshift classroom, I became the teacher and the star pupil, and I learned my lessons well. This training was most assuredly the reason that I spent only a few weeks in kindergarten before being promoted to first grade.

After being promoted to first grade, I wouldn't say anything, and every day during roll call, I cried when my name was called. Each day the teacher called my sister Cynthia out of her class to discover the reason for my tears. At the time, I thought they had changed my class to punish me because I had done something wrong, and being the momma's baby that I was, I cried. This didn't last long, as Cynthia assured me that all was well, that I had become a first grader. Then I quietly enjoyed the challenge.

Influences

We lived in a small town near Woodstock, New York. My dad was an outdoorsman and a sportsman. He enjoyed fishing and hunting, and he always wanted to catch the most fish or bring home the most game from the hunt.

Mom had casually mentioned that he'd played baseball in his youth and that his team had traveled to Clover, Rocky Mount, Gastonia, and other towns on the weekends. That was small-town entertainment at its best. She said that the team played quite a few games after church on Sundays, so the ladies wore their Sunday best and stylish hats and shared rides with fellow enthusiasts.

Their games were social gatherings and a large part of small-town excitement. Fifteen years ago at a family gathering, a friend of the family informed me that my dad had been one of the stars of the team. His goal had been to win and be the league champ. Mom had never shared that bit of information, but now I know where my competitive spirit comes from.

Dad's outdoor activities fascinated us kids, so we tagged along. Each year he planted a garden large enough to share the produce with family and friends. We helped him plant and water his vegetables. He saved potatoes until they began to sprout, and then he cut them into pieces and planted them. To my surprise, we eventually harvested potatoes from them. I wanted to know how could this be. As a kid, I was impressionable and asked lots of questions, to me my dad was a super dad.

When Dad went fishing, we went with him. He brought his radio, prepared to enjoy a Dodgers game. We were happy to accompany him, but we didn't like being in one place very long. We were typical kids and pestered him about going home. He always replied, "In a little while," and then he continued to fish and relax.

As he listened to the Dodgers games on the radio, we became familiar with the game and the players. I'm sure that's why I enjoy baseball today. He taught us how to shoot his rifle and drive his car, which was quite an adventure for a ten-year-old! These actions didn't set well with my mom, but I'm glad he taught us to drive. I love my independence. Mom never learned to drive, so we chauffeured her around.

Baseball became a familiar part of our spring and summer. For quite a few years, Mom and I went to the Mets games. At first we went to Saturday games only, but later we included the Sunday games. Our hotel stay included a room with a view of LaGuardia Airport. We enjoyed a nice prime rib dinner with all the trimmings, watching the planes arrive and depart as we unwound from our busy day activities.

Impressions

It's funny that when we are young we want to imitate everything we see other people do. When I was young, I saw a movie that starred a petite Hollywood skating sensation. She was professionally made up, wore beautiful clothes, lived in a beautiful home, and was naturally the center of attention.

Her main role was to entertain and display many skillful ice-skating maneuvers she had perfected. The scenery was beautiful, her costumes were gorgeous, and she received tremendous applause for her jumps, spins, and twirls.

Well, I thought she was great, and I wanted to do what she did. I had only seen the finished product and had no idea of the long hours she practiced each day to reach her level of excellence. I knew how to skate as a beginner, but I had a long, long way to go to be a polished professional. This was definitely not my gift. I learned to respect, enjoy, and applaud her and others who are accomplished—from a spectator's view.

Without any training, my oldest sister, Lorraine, could draw very well. I would watch in amazement as she'd start with a few squiggly lines and would eventually finish with a beautiful replica of her subject. She even tried to capture her siblings' likenesses, but we were far too active for her to be successful. Naturally, I wanted to draw also, but that wasn't my gift. I didn't have patience for the squiggly lines and many corrections. I wanted to be able to produce the finished, polished product right away.

You know, what we read leaves an impression on us, as it is meant to. A good comedy will make us laugh, a mystery will keep us in suspense, and sorrowful scenes will make us cry or feel sad. We can be happy and joyful when we do what we truly love, and if we can get paid and make a living doing it, that's magnificent. Think about how many radiant, smiling faces you would see each day if we could all be in that situation. Instead of crawling out of bed after hitting the snooze alarm a few times, we would look forward to inventing new ways of bringing creativity into our labor of love. What more could a person want?

Joy in Action

I recall a teacher named Mr. Harvey who, in addition to his daily high school classes, taught adults in the evening. He was a gentle, understanding man and an excellent teacher.

Some of his students enrolled for refresher courses, and others went to get their GED. My mother-in-law, Mrs. Helen Coleman, was one of Mr. Harvey's students. She often commented on the patient and understanding manner with which Mr. Harvey dealt with his students. He recognized their dedication and commitment and assisted in any way he could to help them reach their goals.

I accompanied my mother-in-law to class a few times and witnessed Mr. Harvey's teaching. I was only a visitor, but he didn't let me off the hook—oh, no. He challenged me with questions and problems to solve too! I admired his attitude. He didn't get upset if students didn't remember material that he had previously taught. He made us feel at ease by injecting simple, daily experiences related to the subject at hand. Using sales or discounted percentages encountered in our daily shopping ventures, he illustrated mathematical skills that we were already practicing and equated them to the lesson he was presenting. Mr. Harvey had patience with his students, and patience is a virtue. We are not all so endowed. He was one of the special ones.

Teachers are the means by which knowledge is passed from one generation to the next. To some people, teaching is simply a job, but to those who really care, it's a calling, an opportunity to shape minds and open the windows of our imaginations. Think how blessed teachers and professors are: though they are individuals, they are able to contribute and influence many students throughout years of instruction. They help motivate and enlighten many students, and they themselves lose nothing in the process. They are victors. By passing along what they know, they partake in their students' achievements and success stories. Even if they are never officially recognized, their contributions can never be taken away.

As I was demonstrating my own joy of sharing, I had the chance to witness joy in action. My second week volunteering at Girls Inc. was very rewarding. Six girls between the ages of six and nine had the opportunity to visit the facility of the Association of the Blind. That day's agenda included a demonstration by beginning volunteer dog trainers and their young dogs.

The experience was fascinating. New trainers have to attend weekly classes to learn how to train the puppies or very young dogs they receive. Their obligation consists of many long hours of hard work. Their love of dogs, patience, and contribution make their labor of love awesome. I admire the trainers, for they are part of a worthy cause: assisting visually impaired or blind individuals to get around and maintain their independence.

We witnessed the first stage of the training process. The young dogs were trained to follow orders, interact with people, and know the difference between work time and playtime. Most of the dogs present were Labrador retrievers, among the top choices for service dog work because they are loyal, loving, and highly intelligent. They are also good with children and are easily trained.

What a combination to have young, rambunctious children and dogs in the same room. Most desired to play, have fun, enjoy movement, and interact with each other, but such feelings had to be contained. Believe it or not, everyone behaved!

In addition to the six young girls from Girls Inc., ten attendees of various ages with different degrees of visual impairment also witnessed the demonstrations.

I learned that the dogs wear a harness when they're with a visually impaired or blind person, which indicates that they are working and alert, not playing. They are trained to know the difference. If a guide dog gets away from its owner, the owner pats his own legs and calls the dog's name. The dog is trained to come and sit in front of its owner, so the owner can easily locate it.

The demonstration was fascinating to watch. The trainer, after giving her young dog the command to stay, left him on one side of the room and walked to the other side. When she turned and patted her legs, all the dogs stood ready to respond as they had been trained to do, but only her own dog went to sit in front of her. The young dogs and trainers were very impressive. We had an opportunity to witness the dogs' training and ability to follow orders. Treats were a large part of the training process, which the dogs enjoyed and deserved that day.

Those in attendance who didn't have visual difficulties heard about people who did and how they coped with their daily activities. The visually impaired attendees learned that they could gain help through the trained dogs. Trainers saw the people who would benefit from their hard work. They stated that they felt happy, knowing that they were important and useful and making a difference. To qualify for a guide dog, a person must be able to get around on his own and know where he's going, be over sixteen, and be able to properly care for a dog.

Visually impaired people and Girls Inc. participants received answers to their many questions. We all left feeling well informed. At the end of the session, the Girls Inc. group had the opportunity to interact with the dogs—touching, hugging, and petting them—which they enjoyed. I don't know who enjoyed it more, the girls or the dogs.

I started volunteering at Girls Inc. because I had unfulfilled time on my hands. I only planned on working a few half days, but the trainer's dedication, the program, and the opportunity to be helpful made me consider adding additional time. I wanted to help children learn—especially in reading—but I had a wonderful learning experience myself.

Caregiver's Joy

When my children, David and Deborah, were born, my stay with them in the hospital was a lot longer than what mothers experience today. Back then, we were there long enough to get to know faces and names and a little about the nurses—who woke us up in the middle of the night to get our vital signs or made us get up and walk, whether we wanted to or not.

I always met nice people. My roommate and I had a great time. Our schedule was nonstop. We tried to finish our walk, take a shower, have breakfast, and rest a little while before the next activities began: lunch, more walking, visitors, and so on. Just when we thought we were done, we would hear the squeaky wheels of the mobile cribs delivering our bundles of joy for feeding and mommy time. So much for resting!

There weren't many newborn babies in the nursery, so each mother practically had her own private nurse. One day I was chatting with the young nurse assigned to me. We began talking about our jobs. I worked in an office and enjoyed that kind of work. I asked her why she had chosen nursing. She said that each patient was different, and some had unusual circumstances, but they all needed care. She comforted and held the hands of first-time moms and those who were having physical difficulties as a result of their pregnancies. She was there for those women who had to make snap decisions regarding methods of delivery, for the child's safety or their own. All the while, she assured them that everything would be all right and that their pain would produce one of God's blessed gifts to love and nurture.

The nurse stated that complications could arise at any time, for either the mother or the child. It made her happy to do whatever she could do to ease the pain for the mother, to assist in keeping the newborn breathing on its own, or to incubate the premature babies and monitor their vital signs. At that particular time in her life, she was making a difference to others.

Her joy in giving her time and ability to comfort others and work within unpredictable circumstances is a great example of our individual blessings. She had previously worked in an office, where, if she didn't make it to work, things went on as usual. But as a nurse, she felt that if she didn't make it to work, she would miss the opportunity to assist in one of the most beautiful and blessed features of life: birth. She came in to work early or stayed late if the need arose. At the end of the day, she felt satisfied.

That's what life is all about—making a difference by using your personal source of God-given joy.

Joy, Dedication, and Love for the Game

The New York Giants football team's summer training camp is in our area. As I'm out for my daily stroll, I see the players practicing, some days in the morning and other days in the late afternoon. I've had the opportunity to watch simulated games right in my own backyard.

You can't tell me those dedicated players don't love the game. To suit up in helmets, pads, uniforms, and spiked shoes so they can run around, rain or shine, with temperatures sometimes in the eighties and above, is definite proof. I have seen players sprinting, pushing blocks, and practicing actual plays—all involving exertion.

Some players start fantasizing at an early age about such an experience, visualizing the big game at the end of the season, the Super Bowl, and that coveted prize, the trophy. The Giants' first Super Bowl victory was in 1986, and the last was in 2011.

If this is a person's game, it's invigorating and fun, and it gives him great joy to be on the field. Players who really love the game find ways to participate. Even after their playing days are over, they coach and train others, passing along what they've learned and what has been passed to them. It's an outward expression of their inner love.

How I Found My Joy

Wisdom, gifts, and joy are given by God according to his will.

I started writing this book in order to share how I came to realize my joy. I hadn't been looking for it. As a matter of fact, I had thought I already knew what gave me the most joy. I was surprised to discover that my greatest joy comes from *sharing*! Doesn't that sound simple and unimportant? It's amazing how I arrived at this conclusion.

Life is a journey, and each experience is a stepping stone that brings us closer to our destination and where we are now. In my case, it began with negative actions. I wanted on-the-job training to learn my job, but no one would teach me. Instead, I quickly received an entire day's worth of information, after which I was expected to perform with speed and accuracy in only a few days.

There's a TV program called *Undercover Boss,* where CEOs leave the comforts of home, family, and all the perks they have become used to and go to work, incognito, within their own companies. They are usually trained by an employee who has one to twenty years' experience. Most trainers give their undercover bosses similar evaluations after only a few hours on the job. They say things like:

- They're slow and need to pick up the pace.
- They don't have the stamina for the job.
- They don't remember all the instructions given.
- They can't handle the equipment or registers.
- They won't meet the daily quotas.

I found myself in the identical situation on my first job. I had been promoted to the position of a young lady who was leaving the job to have her first child and was planning to be a stay-at-home mom. Every aspect of her daily work routine was second nature to her, for she had years of experience.

She was quite abrupt with me when I didn't remember her instructions and couldn't dot every *i* and cross every *t* to her satisfaction after a short time on the job. I felt very inadequate and didn't want to consult her on any matter pertaining to the task at hand, but I had to.

When it was my opportunity to train and inform others, I remembered my uneasy training experience, and I tried to be patient and helpful. I even shared all the shortcuts I had discovered. That was the beginning of something that I still try to do: to share what I have learned whenever I can.

Everyone's characters are shaped differently. That's why we can find someone to fulfill every need. At some point in life, when you find your niche, you must, as they say, do your own thing. Those who are gifted with knowledge can teach. Those who love healing can become doctors. Those who have athletic abilities can play sports. Contractors can build. Artists can paint.

Sometimes finding your joy comes from eliminating things you are *not* blessed with the talent or skills to do. If you can't carry a tune, singing is probably not your calling. If you can't stand the sight of blood, I'd say that being a nurse or physician is not your field. If you can't remember lines, follow cues, or change facial expressions for close-up camera scrutiny, acting probably is not for you.

Here is where you might say, "But I love to design," and you could become an interior decorator.

If you can put words into a rhyming pattern to express clear meaning, maybe you could write great poetry. Expressing your inner personal feelings is powerful. We receive many opportunities to demonstrate the gifts that bring us joy.

Don't be stingy with your gift; you only cheat yourself. The great feeling you get is only evident when you share your gift. There will always be someone who has the same gift or talent you have, but there is only one you. No one else has your personal style. Everyone walks, but no one walks quite like you.

So share your gift. Give it away. By all means, make your living from it. Remember that people can't take away your joy unless you allow them to. Just realizing that fact will brighten your day and lift your spirits as you tap into your generous nature.

The Bible says, "It is more blessed to give than to receive" (Acts 20:25).

I've noticed that God has blessed ministers and teachers who study his Word. They come away with a much deeper, clearer understanding than the average person. They are able to unlock the hidden meanings and impart that knowledge to us. But believe it or not, you are exactly who and what God made you to be. We tend to emphasize what we *can't* do, but it's what we *can* do that makes our daily lives meaningful.

Our joy is all wrapped up in our purpose. This is a beautiful package that contains our greatest gift. I no longer feel inadequate as a result of what I can't do or don't know, because I have my own purpose and joy.

And what a thrill it is to be completely at ease and satisfied with my contribution! It's the *sharing* that gives me inner peace and ultimate joy.

When I do what gives me joy, I feel completion and satisfaction, without the need to do or say anything else.

We should live in the present and bloom where we are planted. We should all have dreams and goals of something we look forward to, something we haven't yet achieved, a reason for living. Just take a few minutes to think about what gives you the most satisfaction, makes you happy, warms your heart, and puts a smile on your face. Your joy is probably in the midst of it.

There's a big difference between joy and enjoyment. When you enjoy activities, you are usually a witness. You feel joy when you participate.

There are many things I enjoy. I love to read. It's nice when you can choose any book, sit back, and get lost in the pages. I can be inside on a snowy winter day and read about actions taking place under the warm Tuscan sun, or I can experience the tranquility of someone exploring the coral reef and can imagine the beautiful diversity of fish and swaying sea life in the clear, clean water. Or I can get lost in the twists and turns of a chilling mystery.

I also enjoy traveling, and when I make up my mind that I want to go someplace, I usually don't let anything stop me, even if I have to travel alone. Now that I look back on some of my impulsive actions, I know that God was watching over me.

I decided I wanted to see the Chicago Bulls play at least once before Michael Jordon retired, so I drove alone to Boston on Halloween to see a game. I had been to Boston on a bus trip, but I had never driven. This was a spur-of-the-moment trip. I had no hotel reservation, didn't know where the Boston Garden was located, and didn't have a ticket for the game. But I wanted to go, so off I went.

By the time I got close to Boston, it was rush hour, and traffic began to get heavy. I drove along, wondering how I was going to find the Boston Garden—when I saw an information station.

I entered and asked for direction to the stadium and inquired about nearby hotels and parking. The assistant stated I should stay at a hotel not far from the stadium where parking was included in the nightly rate and take a cab therefore I wouldn't have a parking problem.

My guardian angel was at work again. She gave me directions and told me which exit to take. But wouldn't you know it, I was in the wrong lane, and traffic wouldn't allow me to take the exit. So I was back where I'd started, without a clue as to where I was. I took the next exit and tried to figure out which direction I should be going.

On Halloween in a strange city, you can't ask just anyone for directions, so I figured the next cab driver or policeman would do. Before I had a chance to inquire, I saw one of the main streets the information assistant had mentioned, which eventually led to the hotel. What a relief that was! I was still excited about going to the Boston Garden to see the Bulls play.

My next hurdle was to get a ticket. After going to other arenas, I didn't think that would be a problem. It just usually meant that I would have to sit in the nosebleed section. So I got there, purchased a ticket in the nosebleed section, and proceeded to the first section of seats on the main level immediately off the playing court. My plan was to watch the practice session and take a few pictures. Then I decided to take an unoccupied seat near the court until the rightful owner came.

My plan worked for most of the first quarter. When it was time to move, I explained to the usher that I was alone and had traveled quite a distance to see the game. She was accommodating and showed me to another seat on the same level. The good luck lasted almost to halftime. I went to the snack bar and then to my assigned seat. It was fun! I enjoyed the game, the view, the atmosphere, and every minute of the experience.

I planned to leave before the game ended to eliminate the problem of getting a cab, so going to my assigned seat was okay. The players from that distance looked like little kids. It all worked out. The Bulls won, and I had a nice adventure.

Later, I had another adventure. The Mets had a seven-day trip to Jamaica, where anyone could go along and meet the players and their families. My mom said she would go but was afraid of flying, and she began to get nervous as the time approached. I didn't want anything to happen to her after her first flying experience, so she stayed home and I went alone. I wanted to go on the vacation I had planned. I knew the weather would be nice and warm, for it was early November. It wasn't a long flight, and I would meet new people, relax, go sightseeing, and indulge in a little shopping, all while experiencing the local culture and having fun in the sun.

I had a great time. When I first arrived, most people were in subway-rider mode: facing straight ahead, not making eye contact, and not talking to strangers. But after a short while, the members of the group were looking for each other to have meals together and to enjoy the many activities available. By the end of the week, when group members were leaving, we felt as if we were saying good-bye to old friends, and we really hated to see each other go. We exchanged addresses and phone numbers and actually kept in touch for a while.

A few members of the group were college tennis instructors, which became a large part of our schedule. I even took a few tennis lessons from the hotel instructor. That was different and fun, for tennis is not my game.

One evening, the Mets players, their families, and all members of the group had a formal dinner together, with time allotted for pictures, casual conversations, and autographs.

Our grand evening took place on an upper outdoor terrace with perfect, soft lighting, and we all wore proper evening attire. Our waiters went all-out for the occasion. They wore black tuxedos, bow ties, and cummerbunds as they pulled out our chairs and unfolded our napkins. There was soft music and a warm tropical breeze, and our meal was delicious. It was a scene from one of the many, many books I've read. I wanted to forget reality and stay in paradise forever.

The next day's activity included a softball game, where any member of the group could play along with Daryl, Keith, Jim, and others. I decided to be the photographer. It was a relaxing time compared to the cold weather and busy schedules we had left behind.

Last year I went to see the New York Knicks play an exhibition game against the Boston Celtics at the Times Union Center. Most of the star players from both teams had the night off, but that didn't bother me. I had a chance to see a few of the newest prospects trying to make the team. I didn't have to drive or take a chartered bus to either city to see the game. I had a good seat and saw old friends, and the Knicks won. It was an enjoyable evening.

Going to the Times Union Center to see the arena football games was something else I enjoyed. I've seen the Williams sisters and other pros play in tennis exhibition games at the state university campus, and I've enjoyed seeing the best players up close. Even if I can't get to the main arenas of play, I've still had the opportunity to personally witness their talent.

Seeing Tiger Woods play golf, live and up close, was something I wanted to do, and in 2009 I got my chance. He was playing at the Turning Stone Resort for the Notah Begay III foundation challenge. I had the time of my life. Since it wasn't far away, I drove. My event package included a merchandise gift card,

VIP transportation from the resort to the golf course, a lunch voucher, a free play voucher, and an invitation to a special reception and dinner. It wasn't a sit-down dinner, so I could mingle and sit wherever I wanted to. I must say that they had some of the best prime rib I'd had in a long time. That's one of my favorite foods, which I've never prepared at home but enjoy eating when dining out.

That was my first time attending a golf match of any sort. I'm not a golfer, so there was a lot to capture my attention, and I was excited. The drive was quick and easy, and the weather was ideal. The golf course was beautiful, with water fountains, multicolored flowers, and freshly mowed lawns. There was a limited number of spectators.

At one hole, I watched the players tee off. At another hole, I got near the place where the ball should land, close to the rope that divided the spectators from the real action. Then I was near the green and could see who would sink the moneymaking shot. On one shot, Tiger's ball landed about eight feet away from me. What a Kodak moment—if only we could have brought our cameras!

It was exciting to watch Tiger and his fellow golfers stride down the middle of the course with an estimated twenty-person entourage of news reporters, cameramen, security, and staff members following.

Then I watched him approach his ball and noticed all the different maneuvers he went through before committing to the shot.

We all had the chance to adjust our mental images when we discovered that people looked different in person from the way they looked on TV. I loved Tiger's focus and seriousness on each shot and the sound of the club striking the ball. Needless to say, I had a very enjoyable day.

The aforementioned events were experiences that I enjoyed as I witnessed what others did. But my own joy comes from something I do.

My Sharing

When I was a teenager, I found bowling to be an enjoyable form of entertainment. I was a beginner, and more experienced bowlers instructed me on form and proper placement of the ball on the lanes. They said that right-handed bowlers should roll the ball over the second arrow on the right. Then the ball should hook into the pocket, resulting in a strike, which is the name of the game in bowling. Twelve strikes in a row is a perfect game ... yada, yada, yada.

Needless to say, I tried that formula repeatedly, but to no avail. I was very frustrated, and my companions had no compassion when I couldn't immediately imitate their expertise. My brothers, Robert and

Albert, were good bowlers with averages in the two hundreds, and I wanted to bowl as well as they did.

I began practicing and improved on my own. Believe it or not, I still roll my wrist, even after all these years. It's hard to change old habits, so I live with it. I've had a few six-hundred series in my leagues, so I won't complain.

From my experiences, I have tried to help others improve their games by encouraging them to improve whatever style or form they have. After all, it's the score that counts in the end.

One day while I was practicing, a young couple were bowling a few lanes away from me. He was the better bowler of the two. I could hear him giving her the same complicated instructions I had received, which she couldn't duplicate, either. She had a very low score and threw quite a few gutter balls. How well I remembered being that frustrated and disappointed and not having much fun.

He went to the snack bar, and I couldn't resist helping a fellow bowler. I went over and gave her two simple pieces of advice that usually worked for me. By the third game, he was no longer giving instruction but was doing his best not to let her beat him. It made me feel good to see the smile on her face as her game improved. I left smiling too, happy that my sharing had made a difference in both our lives.

I have spent a great deal of time telling family, friends, coworkers, and everyone I know about finances. This eventually led me to write a pamphlet: "How Anyone Could Save and Live Comfortable Financially." I tried to encourage others to step out, make a few changes, and reap the benefits in their finances. I shared my story of how I'd started with little but had found easy ways to save—and was still able to live comfortably without feeling deprived. Most people I knew were not saving, and they definitely were not in the investment arena. I love helping people change their lives permanently for the good.

As an instructor in the new membership orientation ministry at my church, I have a wonderful feeling after sharing God's Word with the participants. I especially try to encourage everyone to read and study the Bible. There are usually only a few people present, which reminds me of the Scripture that says, "For where two or three are gathered together in my name, there am I in the midst of them" (Matthew 18:20), and I sense God's presence among us.

This is a time when I experience joy. I impart the fact that God has given each of us the gift of salvation, which we must accept. It is a twofold act: God gives, and we accept. Each individual has control of his or her own personal destiny. No one else can make that decision.

I also like to express the secure feeling I get from God's promises: "I will never leave you nor forsake you" (Hebrews 13:5) and "Lo I am with you always" (Matthew 28:20). They remind me that everyone else can and sometimes will leave me, but God's promises make me feel secure, as if I'm wrapped close to him in a warm, cozy, snug blanket.

I remember one particular Saturday at a new membership orientation session. As I was waiting for my assigned class, I was discussing a topic from the lesson with one of my fellow instructors. It was about receiving blessings through testing. Looking at our own lives, we realized how far we had come and how much we had grown spiritually. We had both experienced personal tests when we'd had to demonstrate a loving attitude, even when we were far from feeling that way.

She had learned that a coworker friend she'd confided in had betrayed her to their boss, and she had been let go from her job. The coworker had showed no surprise over the result. My friend's spiritual growth showed in her reaction to the situation. When she encountered her coworker, she apologized to her for putting her in an uncomfortable position. But that's not how she would have handled her problem previously.

I once found myself apologizing to someone who had quit talking to me, even when I didn't know why. I had to reach out and respond in order to right the wrong I might have unknowingly done to cause the situation. Humility is a hard test. It took a few weeks, but I passed my test.

I've had experiences where all I could do was pray about them. Knowing ourselves is very important, and there are times when I need divine intervention to behave in a Christ-like manner.

I was touched that my friend and I had experienced similar situations and that we had grown enough to apologize. We both laughed and shed a few tears over our growth. We also discussed opportunities we had been given in order to demonstrate our love for others.

On another Saturday, I was running late to orientation class. I saw an elderly woman walking slowly up the street toward the church parking lot in a light rain, without an umbrella, scarf, or hat. I rushed into church to let everyone know that I was available for class, but the image of the elderly lady walking in the rain stayed on my mind.

My gift of sharing prompted me to go look for her and give her my umbrella, but she was nowhere to be found. I often think of that, and I know I must do what I can *immediately*. The Bible says a lot about helping others and not forgetting the poor and needy, for it is only by the grace of God that we are not them. I don't know if the woman in the rain was poor, but at that moment, she had been in need.

The Bible says, "But be ye doers of the word, and not hearers only, deceiving your own selves" (James 1:22). God will give us our just reward. Immediate action is my goal.

I feel blessed to be a laborer in God's vineyard, building his kingdom. It is an honor to use his gift of sharing.

Regardless of your age or situation in life, don't be content until you have found your personal, God-given joy.

I have asked a few people from different walks of life to share what gives them the most joy in their personal lives and in their various types of employment. Their stories follow my own.

2

Nadja Pope

Guilderland High School student and Metropolitan NTM Baptist Church youth member

Joy is a feeling you have deep within, when you feel great inside. You should never let anyone steal your happiness and your joy in life. I was always a very happy child and never gave much thought to not being happy. Life offers many opportunities that give me joy. God has blessed me many times and has given me many opportunities that some people haven't experienced.

One of those opportunities is the ability to go to a place of worship and worship freely. I have been in church all my life and love my church family. I have friends at church, and the church members are very loving and welcoming. I enjoy coming into the church and feeling a positive and loving vibe.

I also have the chance to go to Sunday school and receive a great lesson. Sunday school has taught me to be obedient and responsible. It has also changed me because I have learned to love and care for others in a Christian way. I have been taught that I am able to give because God has blessed me and given so much to me, and I must use those blessings to be a blessing to others.

Seeing my friends on Sunday brings me joy. We have a chance to chat and catch up on all the things that have happened during the week. In our church, there are many unique ministries, and I am free to participate and worship the Lord in these ministries. I also have a wonderful pastor who is very supportive of the youth in the church. He is an incredible preacher, and he truly loves the Lord.

I find joy in helping those who may have less than I have or may just need a little help, especially when children are involved. I have always been taught to share. I plan to help in the annual equinox Thanksgiving dinner this year as another way of giving back. We are usually blessed with more than we need for Thanksgiving dinner, and I want to help someone who may not be in the same position.

Being involved in the community and doing volunteer work is something I enjoy. Helping others gives me a good feeling because I know I have done the right thing for someone else. I feel I'm making a contribution to the world in my own small way. I have a chance to help make the world a better place, and being around positive role models helps me become a positive role model.

Volunteering has given me joy by allowing me to give to others, to work with people with different personalities, to build many useful skills that will help me in the future, to build my confidence, and to meet new people and learn new things. Just doing one little thing can make a big difference, and that gives me satisfaction. There are many issues going on in our society that involve young adults, and when I volunteer, I work hard and do my best so that when I'm finished, I know I have left a positive impression.

In the summer of 2013, I had a great opportunity to go to Europe, where I traveled to Spain, France, and Italy. I had an amazing time and got to see many famous places that I had previously only read about or seen on television: the Leaning Tower of Pisa, the Colosseum, the statue of *David*, the Trevi Fountain, the Sistine Chapel, and the Rhone American Cemetery.

This trip was really the experience of a lifetime. I was away from home for three weeks, and I got to learn about three different cultures and lifestyles, tasted many new and different foods, cooked great meals, built my self-confidence, and made lots of new, lasting friendships. I will never forget my trip, and I'm very grateful to have had such an opportunity.

My family also brings me joy. I have a very loving and supportive family. My mom and grandmother are there for me always. Whether I give a dance performance, receive an award, or need help with something, they have my back, no matter what. I thank God every day for them. They want me to be the best in everything I do. They push me hard to do my very best, even when I don't want to, but in the end I thank them because my parents know what's best.

My mom has a wonderful personality, and being with her brings me lots of laughter and fun times. She always has a smile on her face, is very kind and gentle, and has passion for everything she does. I love my mom, and I tell her every day. We spend a lot of mother-and-daughter bonding time—at the movies, cooking, or just sitting and talking and laughing about things. She provides me with support, guidance, and structure.

My grandmother is a phenomenal woman. She has room in her heart for everyone. If someone needs her, she will be there. Anything a person needs her to do, she will do. I like to go shopping and traveling with my "G'ma." We are alike in our personalities and have good times together. We like to go everywhere, and with every new adventure, we learn something new. She is an excellent cook and always prepares whatever I want. She probably spoils me a little, but I guess that's what grandmothers are supposed to do.

This year has started off different from the norm for me. After going on my trip abroad, I see things in a new way. I now know that every day and every situation is a new learning experience. I get to dig deeper in life, see more and do more exciting things every chance I get. I am very grateful to be able to get an education, for there are many places in the world where children are not allowed to do so.

I work hard in school, knowing it will pay off now and in the future. I enjoy the challenges and rewards of high school and the activities that I am able to participate in. My high school and college education will give me the opportunity to be successful and independent.

Joy is something I never thought about until I was asked to, and then I realized that my happiness and joy came in many ways and many forms—church involvement, personal family time, volunteering, and even my schooling. I am a happy person because it is all I've ever known. Being unhappy or sad has no place in this temple.

Nadja Gore

3

Clifford James Avery

**Christian Brother Academy student and
Metropolitan NTM Baptist Church youth member**

There are many things that bring me joy, like going
to see a movie or having fun with family and friends.
But the joy that God has given me is much different.
The Lord has blessed me with the ability to make

other people smile. When I smile, it seems to brighten some people's days. I am a member of the junior usher board at my church, and I enjoy greeting members and visitors with a smile. When I do, it makes that person smile back.

My parents always make sure I get to school on time, finish my assignments, and try to get good grades. As a result, I can also enjoy the sporting activities at my school. I enjoy running and am a member of the track team. Our school has a pretty good team. I had the opportunity to travel with the team and visit many schools, and I was one of the ten qualifiers who traveled to Yale University for a track meet. We were all excited to go, as it was the first time for most of us to visit Yale.

We didn't get to see much of the campus, but their track was the best I'd ever run on. The surf was banked, which made running easy. We were happy when our team won the 4x200-meter relay race.

This year I am also on the football team as a free safety and running back. Being a member of the track team helped prepare me for these positions. Our team has a lot of fun, even though we have to work and train very hard. We won our super bowl this year, but we were eliminated in the first round of state qualifying. We learned a lot but are still looking for our first state championship.

As I look ahead to college, I hope my running time is fast enough to help me receive letters from colleges offering scholarships in track and field. A few of my choices would be Louisiana State University, Florida State, or Syracuse University. I am training with a personal trainer in hopes of going to the Olympics in track and field, which would also give me a chance to travel. Some of my favorite runners are Usaine Bolt and Yihan Blake. They run the same events I do, and they have great forms, which I would like to learn. My running time last year was very close to Usaine Bolt's, which allows me to dream, for he is the fastest runner at the present time.

Another thing that God gave me that gives me joy is the ability to make music. Playing music allows me to express my emotions through song. At the church I attend, I play the drums for various choirs, and when I am playing, I feel that I am expressing myself to God through the beat of the drums. I also play the saxophone at my church in a horn group called the Metro Horns. The group only plays gospel music. When playing the saxophone, I feel even more connected with God because I know that God gave me the musical talent to play the instrument. When playing the saxophone at church, I put my best foot forward and put soul into the tone of the horn to make it almost sing and sound smooth.

God has blessed me with so much throughout my life, and there is no way I can ever repay him. I try my hardest to express myself to him, not just through prayer but through my God-given abilities to bring joy to other people, and to myself, through playing the drums and the saxophone.

Clifford J. Ames

4

Preston Martin T. Butler

Guilderland High School student and Metropolitan NTM Baptist Church youth member

Dogs bring me more joy than anything else in my life ever has.

Can I please get one? That was the question I constantly asked my mother throughout my younger years. I had begged my heart out for a dog for as long as I could remember. I had pleaded for years, only to be shut down with a consistent reply: no.

But I didn't let that discourage me. For four years I prayed to God for the dog of my dreams, and I never once let the Devil steal my joy.

When I was five years old, the Lord had blessed me with a wonderful puppy named Chewy. He was a white pit bull with a brown spot on his left thigh, and he didn't have a killer bone in his body. It was summertime when my father brought him home. Sadly, my father worked nights and could not take care of Chewy at all. I was too young to properly take care of him, and he was too much for my mother to care for at the time. So, after only two weeks of having my best friend, he was taken away. That was the day I asked God to please bless me with another dog— when I would be able to take care of it.

During the next ten years, we moved three times. When I was six years old, we moved to an apartment complex and stayed there until I was eight. When we first moved there, I asked my mom if we could get a dog, but she said the apartment complex didn't allow pets. I remained hopeful that I would get a dog someday and that this was just a bump in the road.

When I was eight, we moved to a cozy little white house, and I asked again: "Can we get a dog, please?"

This time it was not a complete shutdown. My mother said that once we got settled she would think about it. Those words brought me so much joy that I took on almost all of the chores around the house.

I was already very active in our church: singing in the youth choir, being a member of the youth usher board, and attending Sunday school. I have always enjoyed school—especially math and science. I realized at an early age the importance of getting excellent grades in school. Even though I had picked up extra chores around the house, I knew that if I continued to do exceptional work in school and stay at the top of my class with good grades, my mom would one day let me have that puppy.

After one year, we still didn't have a dog. I asked my mother my favorite question once more, and this time she said we could not afford a dog right then. I stayed joyful and optimistic. I thought that if I could not have a dog, I would get a different pet for the time being. My father and I went to the mall and picked up my first hermit crabs. Their names were Tony and Russ, and they were only the first of seven that I would have.

Two years later, we moved again—still without a dog. The new apartment complex, thank God, allowed pets. I did not ask my mother for a dog for two years. Instead, over that two-year period, I had four hamsters, a turtle, five fish, and two more hermit crabs. I was hopeful that when I asked for a dog this time, the answer would be yes. She had been tolerant toward all the pets I'd had in the past two years, and I had been able to show her that I was responsible in caring for them. Sure enough, when I asked the question, she said she would seriously consider it.

The fire of longing that had once burned inside of me for a dog had begun to fade. But my mom's words added thousands of coals to the fire, and it burned brighter than ever. By that time, I was twelve, and I was the happiest I had ever been in my life. I began looking online for local shelters that had pit bull puppies. I still had not forgotten about my first pal, Chewy.

One day, I was watching my favorite TV show, *Dog Whisperer*. Cesar Millan had just gotten a new pit bull puppy named Junior. It was a beautiful gray pup with white paws. At that moment, I knew it was the type of dog I wanted.

I had lunch with the superintendent of my church Sunday school, and we were talking about dogs. She had a German shepherd that she had trained by using Cesar Millan's book. When she asked if I wanted to borrow the book to learn how to train a puppy, I knew that this was another sign from God that my prayers would be answered.

I began to pray every day for the dog I'd seen on that TV show. We had family prayer every night before we went to bed, and I always prayed for the pit bull I wanted. Although my mother and sister prayed against the idea, I did not let that discourage me. I knew God would be faithful to me, so I kept praying and believing in his Word. Year after year, I prayed— until God answered my prayer when I turned fifteen. My father's friend's pit bull had just birthed a litter of puppies, and I asked my mom if we could go see them. To my astonishment, she actually said yes!

With that, we went to look at the litter. They were all beautiful, and they were every color I could imagine. I saw several that I wanted, but every time I picked one, the owner said that it had already been promised to someone else.

Then I found one puppy that was off to the side. It was the spitting image of what I had asked God for. I immediately knew that he had been waiting for me. I picked him up and said to my mother, "He's the one." She knew he was the one also, because he was exactly what I had been praying for all those years. She asked the owners when we could come to take the puppy home.

We brought him home three weeks later. I named him Poseidon because he had the bluest eyes I had ever seen. Everyone said, "You know, his eyes are going to change," but they are still aqua-blue a year and a half later.

I enjoy many things: my family, my church family, friends, and school. I have received academic awards, and I had the opportunity to be one of a chosen few who attended a week of workshops at Rensselaer Polytechnic Institute last summer. This year I will travel to Washington, DC, to attend additional educational workshops. But my real joy comes from interacting with Poseidon, for there are no conditions placed on our relationship, only the freedom to have fun.

My dog brings me joy in so many ways. He helps relieve my stress. Before I got Poseidon, I frequently had awful migraine headaches, but since I got him, I don't have them as often. Now, if I find myself getting stressed, I think about him and anticipate going for a long walk in the woods and not having a worry in the world.

I enjoy sports, and they require that I do a lot of running. If Poseidon and I are out for a run and I begin to slow down, he will tug on his leash as if to say, "You can keep going." The greatest joy of all is knowing that he is always there to cheer me up. It seems that he can sense when I am feeling down. Then he comes and snuggles next to me, which is a great comfort, and I enjoy his nearness.

I thank God—and my parents—for giving me the one thing that my heart desired, for my dog has brought me so much joy!

Pastor Martin J. Butler

5

Christine B. Teal, MD

Director of Breast Care Center, associate professor of surgery, George Washington University Medical Faculty Associates

When I watch my children, I often worry about worst-case scenarios. If they are limping, could it be a bone tumor? If they have swollen lymph glands, could it be lymphoma? If their belly hurts, is it appendicitis?

And then I transport myself back to reality. Their leg just hurts, a virus has caused swollen lymph nodes, and they just have a bellyache.

But when my amazing tabby cat, Tigger, started limping, my sixth sense set in, as it does so often with my patients, and I knew it was cancer. My daughter, Ashley, who also has a sixth sense, knew it as well. I wanted to wait until after the weekend to take him in because I didn't want to ruin our weekend trip away, but Ashley refused to go if I didn't take him in.

The x-ray confirmed what I knew already: Tigger had an osteosarcoma of his left leg and would need an amputation. I felt a deep sadness for him in his pain and suffering, and I was frustrated that I couldn't explain it to him. I was afraid of what was to come, even more than I'd been when I'd had my own surgery—bilateral prophylactic mastectomies. I suspect it was because of the unknown.

My own surgery had been very familiar to me. I had performed it often on my own patients. I thought I knew all about it and what to expect. But I learned from my own surgery that I hadn't truly known what my patients went through; I only thought I'd known. I also learned that I will never know what it is like to be told that I have breast cancer. I am thankful to be able to avoid that journey myself, but I feel fortunate that I am in a position to help others through it.

Every day I share cancer news with women who are often very young. Most of the time, I can't explain to them why they got breast cancer. I can't say I know their fear, because I have never been told that I have breast cancer. But I understand and can relate because of my personal experiences with it. Having watched my mother go through it twice and my best friend three times, I went through my own surgery to be sure I never heard the words, "You have breast cancer." I have an idea of what these women's journeys will involve. Some of them will be more difficult than others, and some women will handle their experience better than others. What makes me feel so blessed is that I get to be part of that journey and guide my patients through it.

When I was a medical student, I knew I wanted to go into surgery. Even before medical school, I knew it. I was going to be a hard-core surgeon—and maybe even be too busy to have a husband or kids. When I was a resident, I was sure I wouldn't go into a breast specialty. It made me too sad to take care of young women with breast cancer. When I was rotating on the breast surgery service at Memorial Sloan Kettering, I cried at the end of many days.

When I graduated from residency in the summer of 1997, I went to Andrews AFB as a military surgeon to pay back my four years of medical school. I was excited to do general surgery and didn't think much about focusing on breast cancer. All of that changed in the fall of 1997. My mother was diagnosed in November and my best friend in December. Taking care of women with breast cancer became my calling.

When my mother was diagnosed the first time, it was all so straightforward that I didn't worry terribly. (It was much different the second time.) She had breast conservation surgery, followed by radiation and then tamoxifen. I felt the impact of having a family history of breast cancer, but otherwise it was not overly stressful.

It was an entirely different experience with my friend Laurie. She was only thirty-four, and her father had died from breast cancer. I watched my strong friend completely fall apart. She was sure she was going to die just as he had. But then something amazing happened to her. She decided that she was not going to be her father that she was going to beat this.

She got through chemotherapy and broke up with her boyfriend of five years, who wouldn't commit to her. She knew she needed someone better, and in 2001 she found the man I consider her angel. At one point, she told me she was afraid that God had put him in her life to help her if the cancer came back. She reasoned that if she didn't let him into her life, the cancer wouldn't return. I told her that was ridiculous, but my sixth sense knew she was right.

She married him in 2004, and a year later, she was diagnosed with recurrent cancer. How could this be? She had finally found happiness, but again she had to face chemotherapy, radiation, and later on, bilateral mastectomies. Life can be so cruel and unfair. But she did it again with a strength and resilience I'm not sure I would have had—with her wonderful husband at her side. Laurie never ceases to amaze me and almost never asks "why me?" I am so proud of her and feel so lucky to be her friend.

I see that kind of strength so often in my patients. Initially, they think they can't handle it, and yet with an amazing grace, they do, and they come through it all even stronger than they were.

I saw it with my mother when she was diagnosed with breast cancer for a second time. We had just walked the Race for the Cure in Washington, DC, in June 2010. She called me a couple of days later because she'd forgotten to show me a lump under her arm. But it was under her right arm, and the cancer in 1997 had been in the left breast, so I didn't think much of it. I told her to get an ultrasound and a needle biopsy.

A few days later, she called me with that sound in her voice that the news was not good. A mammogram and ultrasound did not show anything, but an MRI had found the cancer. She had both breasts removed, as well as the lymph nodes under her arm. How could that be? I knew the road ahead was going to be a rough one. But just as Laurie had amazed me with her strength, my mother did the same.

A couple of days after the surgery, I caught her pulling weeds from my garden and driving to the store. I told her that we don't allow our patients to drive when they are just a few days out of surgery. She asked, "Why not?" and ignored my advice. She went home to Pennsylvania for chemotherapy and kept up her usual busy life of bridge, dinners with the ladies, theater, and taking care of my father. She amazed me, just as Laurie had.

I've learned that a diagnosis of breast cancer means a different journey for each patient. For some, it is just a blip in their lives, and for others, it is a life-changing event. I have learned so much from Laurie and my mother: how to handle it and how it can affect everyone's life. I learn more about myself with each journey I share with my patients. I feel so honored that they and their family members trust me with their care. If I can help just a little—and not just the surgical aspect of it—then I know I have done so much. I feel fortunate that I get to be a part of their lives, that I can be with them when they are so scared and can help them to have the strength to get through it all.

I feel joy every day on my drive home, for I know I have studied every patient's chart thoroughly and have contemplated every possible solution for her condition. I have given 100 percent of my effort. And with all the new technology used for detecting and treating cancer, we are getting closer and closer to a cure.

I look forward to the day when the announcement is made that the "Race for the Cure" is no longer a dream but a reality. My joy will be complete when I can pass along the good news to all the women, young and old, whose lives have been in turmoil because of their battle for an uncertain future. Then I can relax and peacefully enjoy the ride home to once again experience the joy of my family. What an amazing journey for me!

CBTeal

6

Julie DeFruscio

Co-owner and president of Pump Wear Inc. and diabetes awareness and insulin pump accessory specialist

It's funny when I think about what gives me joy now, compared to what I thought it was years ago. I used to work nonstop while raising a family of three very active children. I used to think that having a great family and a job I loved—basically, having it all—was my joy. I was so wrong. Twelve years ago, I discovered what real joy was.

My joy started when my daughter Nikki, then two and a half years old, was diagnosed with type 1 diabetes. Many of you would ask me how I can think of a devastating disease as a joy, and you would be right. I can't. But what the diagnosis brought into my life became my joy.

There are many people around us who are so busy plowing through life that they truly forget to live it. I was one of those people, trying to get it all done, trying to have everything perfect. Anyone who has lived with diabetes can attest to the fact that there is nothing perfect about it. There is also no absolute way to manage diabetes, so having a daughter battle this illness really threw my world upside down.

I began to realize my joy when I could finally slow down and appreciate the simplest of things, like holding a sleeping baby. It no longer mattered that the boss wanted me to work ten- and twelve-hour days, or that the extra money would mean I could remodel the kitchen. My joy began to manifest in sharing many special moments with my daughter as she struggled to gain control of this devastating disease. I realized at that time that although people understood my plight, they wanted me to eventually get over it!

With type 1 diabetes, you can't simply get over it. It lives with you, twenty-four seven. Although I knew that many people felt for me, they didn't truly get the gist of this illness. But I did; I was living it. During that time, I began to understand that I would have to become my daughter's advocate. I would have to find a way to give her some of my joy. A new feeling of finally understanding what was really important in life was my true joy, and I wanted her to share in that as well.

As she grew, I made many changes. I slowed down and began to smell the roses. I know that's an old saying, but it's exactly what I did. With my new understanding, I was better able to focus on what Nikki truly needed. When her two brothers were also diagnosed with diabetes two years later, I was much better prepared. I believe that God gives us all obstacles to overcome, and how we meet each obstacle can make or break us.

I choose to live my joy. My children have brought me more joy than anything in this world. A night out to dinner with my son is greater by far than running home from work to do the dishes or laundry. I am blessed to have a husband who, I think, has always known what his joy is, and I have reaped the benefits.

I have tried to teach my children that the key to joy is in having a positive attitude. Finding the positive in everything will give us much happiness, and I truly believe that it has.

My son once asked, "How can you be positive about diabetes?" My response was, "It's okay to hate the disease, but be thankful that you have something you can try to control. Be thankful for all the new technology that helps you manage your diabetes today. Above everything else, be thankful that you have insulin—and the joy of living.

Through the years, I've met many families affected by diabetes, and our family has participated in numerous walks for a cure. We have established a "Caring & Sharing" weekend for those families, where we bring together over twenty families—yes, entire families—just to bond and regroup. This weekend is about the *joy of life* and the blessing of having each other. I've become a spokesperson to promote awareness, and I have traveled all across the country, even to Washington, to lobby for more research and funds to find a cure for diabetes.

I'm willing to do anything I can to help. An outcome of my involvement has been the start of a business called Pump Wear Inc. that keeps everyone up to date, aware, and informed about diabetes. We also started an outreach business called Girly Girls Studio, inspired by my daughter. We make fun, fashionable handbags and accessories for diabetic girls and ladies to carry necessary monitoring equipment. All of this is meant to lift their spirits and allow them to be stylish as well.

Today, at the age of fifty-three, I'm so happy that I've been able to find joy in just living my life. A nice walk in the park with my daughter, a night out with my son, and the presence of a new daughter-in-law are all blessings I enjoy. I've even begun running, and I enjoy that also. When I run in a race, it's not about coming in first. It's about being in the race and crossing the finish line. Life is too short, and it's really all about living in the moment and enjoying that new bud on the rose bush.

I think my joy became even clearer to me when my father died five years ago. He had been ill and lived in a nursing home. After he passed away, we went to remove his belongings from the facility and found that basically his whole life had been stored in one box. In it were photos of all of us—his grandchildren and his wife. There were no materialistic items, only memories that he had wanted with him. I think that made me really aware of true joy, and I understood exactly what I wanted to be in the box of my own life.

People have often told me that I'm always positive and upbeat. I hope I am and that I am able to share it with others. Someone once said to me, "It won't be your boss standing by your bedside in your last moments. Think of the people who will be there for you. Enjoy them every day, and you will truly have joy.

7

Juanita M. Palmer-Diggs

Registered child-care provider

I absolutely love the career I've chosen as a child-care provider. It's very fulfilling and rewarding in many ways. I initially pursued a career in the corporate world, only to find that my passion is in enriching the lives of children.

My mother gave birth to four children, three girls and one boy. I was the firstborn, and at a very early age, I found myself taking on a huge responsibility with my siblings. I was their caregiver, and I assisted daily with their hygiene, meals, getting dressed, and doing homework.

After graduating from high school, I went off to college to study communications. Following college, my first job was with IBM as a customer service representative. I loved my job and the work, but I felt that something was missing. So I searched for another job.

I took a position at Albany Medical Center Hospital as a receptionist. I loved the staff, my work, and the interaction with people, but I continued to feel empty inside. As the years passed, I gave birth to my daughter, placed her in day care, and returned to work. My heart was crushed. Two years later, the department I worked for relocated out of state.

At that point, I looked for a job that I thought would be rewarding and satisfying. I settled for a position with Amtrak as a customer service representative. I was happy for the job, but I was not settled in my heart. After a year in this position, I was injured and was placed on medical leave.

It was during that time that I could think and reflect. In doing so, I realized how content I was being home with my daughter, who was then two years old. I had the privilege of teaching, enriching, and spending quality time with her. This time also allowed me to reflect back on my own childhood days when I'd cared for my siblings. How exciting that had been!

As I pondered this, my heart leaped with joy. I was sure of my direction. I wanted to become a registered child-care provider and work from my home. This is how my career began.

I met the New York State requirements to become a registered child-care provider. I took training to learn how to care for children from ages six weeks to twelve years. To my surprise, there was a lot to learn!

As a registered child-care provider, I had to separate my parenting skills, childhood influences, and experiences and become an expert in the field of child care. I learned to be intentional with each child placed in my care. It was not only about the paycheck; it was an opportunity to provide a service and to make a tangible difference in the children's lives. I have the chance to be one of the children's first teachers outside of their family.

I have received countless hours of training as a registered child-care provider in: statutes and regulations (pertaining to child day care), childhood development (including appropriate supervision of children and meeting each child's need with physical or emotional challenges and behavior management and discipline), child-care program development (curriculum that encompasses all four developmental domains: physical, social, emotional, and cognitive), safety and security (including communication with parents), business administration (keeping of accurate records and files pertaining to day care), nutrition (sanitation and education on healthy eating), health (including medical treatment and prevention of the spread of disease), and child abuse and maltreatment (identification and prevention).

I am as passionate about my career today as I was sixteen years ago when I started. The good thing about caring for children is that the benefits are not one sided. I get to laugh, love, and learn every day I am with them. I love children, and passing on my knowledge to them is important to me. Being a caregiver teaches me how to be more compassionate, dedicated, patient, and knowledgeable, and I am a positive role model for them.

This career has definitely fulfilled my heart's desire. Loving, nurturing, teaching, cuddling, and disciplining are all part of my work—and more. Through the years, I have witnessed the joy of my labor and have found it to be very rewarding.

J. M. Diggs

8

Dwane J. Grant

NYSP investigator sergeant, musician and minister of music at Metropolitan NTM Baptist Church

Since as far back as I can remember, music has drawn me like steel to a magnet. I've gravitated toward the tonality of the instrument and voice since my early childhood years.

In the home where I grew up, someone was always playing music. I heard music being played on the radio. I heard music being sung around the house. I heard music being played on the piano. Throughout my home, I heard music.

While most of my friends spent their evenings or weekends enjoying outdoor activities, I sat through choir rehearsals, listening, watching, absorbing, and learning music. Back then, I didn't realize how paramount music was in my life. But looking at where I am today, I can say with undeniable confidence that music is a prevailing and influential factor in my life.

My father was anointed with the gift of music and has been mastering the art his entire life. For years I watched him practice on the keys and teach notes and harmonies to choirs. I sat in amazement as he listened to music and reproduced it, adding his own personal flare, which was usually better than the original recording.

I watched his hands glide over the keys of the piano and took note of the way he slid his foot along the pedals of the organ. I listened to him give notes to the sections of the choir under his direction, and I was awed by the way the notes seemed to blend seamlessly.

My mother was no less instrumental in my musical development. To the surprise of many, she was also musically inclined. Having been professionally trained on her instrument, she was able to provide me with a great deal of instruction, and I acquired an abundance of information and skill from her.

After I'd watched and learned from my father, it was my mother who insisted that I spend time sitting at the piano and practicing my finger placement and discipline. I can still picture myself sitting at the piano with my mother by my side as I played a piece of music to the rhythm of her wooden, wind-up metronome.

I have always been in love with music—*all* genres of music.

The smooth sounds of jazz helped get me through many study sessions throughout my college years. The elegant style of the timeless classical pieces provided me with a calm that was needed during stressful points in my life. The stories told in blues and country music always provided me with a personal connection to the song. Listening to the electric guitar solos of the rock genre tickled the adventurous side of me. But gospel music seemed to have a bit of it all. Gospel music always seemed to capture my attention, as I would spend hours and hours playing the same song over and over.

All the music I heard, no matter the genre, seemed to have an affect on me. The affect was at various times soothing, numbing, and invigorating.

Most of all, I enjoy listening to and working with other musicians. Every time I sit down with a group of musicians and listen to their creativity, I get inspired. It never ceases to amaze me how other musicians can hear the same piece of music and make it sound completely different from what I hear. I am forever learning from them, and my style is always evolving as a result.

I am blessed to have been touched with just a small portion of the skill and anointing of my parents' musical abilities. I have always given my skill and talent back to God, and I will continue to do so for as long as he gives me the strength.

I've enjoy many years of service with the New York State Police, and I was recently promoted to investor sergeant, which I am happy about. But of all life's blessings, music is my joy.

9

Michael A. Hairston

CEO of Michael A. Hairston Fine Art & Custom Framing

In college I was a pre-med major and played football and baseball at Hampton University and Howard University. I had aspirations of either going to medical school or playing professional sports. After college, a former teammate introduced me to Adolphus Ealey, the premier black art dealer in the country. This was a stepping stone for me and an introduction into the world of fine art.

Mr. Ealey taught me how to distinguish the difference between fine art and all other expressions of art. As a result of this introduction, I began to paint, and under his tutelage, I attempted to make a legitimate contribution to the world of art. To date, I have approximately 107 original works in private homes and corporate offices throughout the country.

In 1988, I answered an ad in the newspaper for a box-framing position at a commercial framing company. There I met Steven Frizalone, a sales representative who owned What's in a Frame, a black art and custom framing business. He and I became good friends and realized that we had a lot in common. Interestingly, he was Italian American, and he had started one of the first African-American art businesses on the east coast. I left the box-framing company and worked full time with Steve at his business.

I started out as a framer, and later I became a manager, district manager, and finally, a partner. I helped his company expand from three stores to eleven stores in the Washington metropolitan area. We had a great run, and it was extremely rewarding. Steve is one of the smartest people I know, and I would later use his business model for my own company. Unfortunately, in 1994 the party was over, and we went our separate ways. However, to this day, we remain friends.

In 1995, I started Michael A. Hairston Fine Art & Custom Framing, located in downtown Silver Spring, Maryland. We have been at this location for nineteen years.

Initially, my mother and I were going to run the store, but I soon realized that it was too much for her to handle. My father retired from NASA after thirty-six years as an aerospace engineer and rocket scientist, and he immediately came on board with me to run the store. He is the most overqualified framer on the planet.

We have a family business that has employed many people throughout the years, and recently my daughter has also come on board. Being a small family business, our customers truly appreciate us, as we do them. We are not a box store in any way, shape, or form. We are part of the local community and have been for many years. We have developed our clientele, which consists of cleaning ladies, professional athletes, judges, lawyers, politicians, nuns, and everyone else. All are welcome.

My company's slogan is "We make everything beautiful," and this is what we do, day in and day out.

We have framed shoes, pictures, original paintings, jerseys, documents, flags, and a toilet seat!

We take great pride in putting smiles on people's faces, whether it is a grandmother framing her grandson's degree or a loved one framing a deceased family member's photo. What we do may not be of life-or-death importance, but it is extremely important to the clients who walk through our doors.

As rewarding as it is to run my own business, it is also very stressful. It requires a commitment of twenty-five hours a day, eight days a week. It is not for everybody. I have been interviewed on many occasions—once or twice on television. During these interviews, I have been asked whether I would rather do anything else. The answer is no. I adore what I do. No two days are ever the same, and the joy that our work brings to our clients is priceless.

I am truly thankful and blessed that my joy comes from being in the position I am in today, and I look forward to tomorrow with great anticipation.

Michael A. Hairston

10

George H. Hoffman

Proprietor of Sunset Recreation Bowling Center

When people talk about good fortune, I think I'm a perfect example. I am the proprietor of Sunset Lanes in Albany, New York. It's a business that my father handed down to me in 1983, and I truly enjoy running it. He inherited the business from his father when he passed away. My grandfather started the business in 1940. Prior to that, he had been an iceman. Along with his eight brothers, they had peddled ice and made a lot of money in the business. But they had realized that refrigeration was coming, and they thought they should start their own business.

My grandfather became a bowling alley operator, and he started with sixteen lanes. As bowling became more popular, he added eight additional lanes in 1951. When it became even more popular—and the automatic pinsetters came and the pin boys left—he added eight more lanes, which gave us a thirty-two-lane bowling alley. We have a split house—sixteen lanes in the front and sixteen in the back. This arrangement has worked very well over the years.

After I'd worked for UPS for fifteen years, my father asked me in 1983 if I would help him run the bowling business. We worked together until he retired three years later, and then he handed it over to me. Now I call that good fortune!

It was a family-run business, and my mother worked the desk for my grandfather, for my father, and then for me after I took over. She didn't bowl or keep score. She was more of a "people" person, and she kept the place spotless, a practice I try to continue.

When I ran the business on my own, I ran it the way I wanted to. I had tried to change things with my father, but we'd had different ideas.

When I started out, I had no overhead. I didn't owe anybody any money, and I even had a house without a mortgage. So I came in with the idea that I was going to fix the place up. Over the years, I've invested a lot of money. In 1995, I took out a six-hundred-thousand-dollar loan and did a major renovation. I hadn't been in debt before, but I sure got in debt quickly! I turned the business from a bowling alley to a bowling center. I don't know if the business overtook me or I overtook the business, but I became very involved to make it successful.

It wasn't as easy as it seemed to be when other people did it. I couldn't just open the doors and watch people float in. I had to do a lot more promotional things—advertising and things of that nature—which I've learned to do. Especially now, in the computer age, it's necessary to use mobile websites and have our own website. I've done all these things to keep the business going. A lot of bowling centers have failed over the last twenty-five years. We've been successful and will try to remain that way.

I truly enjoy the business, and I can put my own personal stamp on it. Everybody thinks it's a blue-collar place, but doctors, athletes, and many prominent people bowl here. I meet all sorts of nice people, which is great for when I have a problem. There's usually someone who bowls here who can come to my rescue.

My business is definitely not about money anymore. I don't make that much. It's more about the idea that it's my home away from home, a chance to do what I love doing. I spend more time here than I do at my regular home. When I get here, I feel very comfortable. It has never felt like a day of work for me. If I come in at eight in the morning and stay until midnight, I never look back and say, "Wow, I stayed here sixteen hours today." I never give it a thought. Sometimes I work three hours and then go home. I can leave, as long as everything is covered. I've been fortunate to have very good employees. They're the backbone of any business. Mine are reliable, capable, and eager to make the bowling experience enjoyable for everyone, whether I'm there or not.

Providing a place for family enjoyment has been a seven-days-a-week commitment. It used to be open three hundred and sixty-five days a year. When my father and grandfather ran the business, they never closed for holidays. Now we're closed Christmas Eve, Christmas Day, Memorial Day (because I'm a veteran), and the Fourth of July. Holidays are good for business, and a lot of families like to come and open bowl and spend an enjoyable day together.

Another part of our business is the tavern, which my father never ran. I took that over when I came in. I always look for ways to expand, grow, and improve to stay competitive. It's a separate business, which has been a bonus for us also. We added a snack bar that serves quality food that people enjoy. We have great pizza and chicken wings, so I'm told.

Real joy comes from reaching out, in-house and in the community. I've organized a tournament every year called the In-House Tournament, which is where I really see many of our regular bowlers. With pride and joy, I get to stand on the approach and greet everyone. The tournament runs for over thirty nights, and there are eighty people on a squad. We usually have a theme, and I dress up as someone from a particular era. We have music, raffles, lots of food, and a good time. And everyone leaves with a prize.

I'm proud that through the bowling center we've done benefits for some of the catastrophes that have happened in the world in the past few years. We raised thousands of dollars for Haiti and Hurricane Irene, and we raised over eleven thousand dollars for Hurricane Sandy down in New Jersey, New York, and Staten Island areas. I throw a tournament together, and all these good people graciously respond. It's the clientele that come into this bowling center who make it happen. When asked to jump aboard, they do, and we all help out.

My life has been made better by the variety of people I've met. I'm sixty-eight now, and I would like to stay until I'm seventy. But if someone comes along and offers me about fifty million dollars, I might sell. Otherwise, I'll probably be here until I'm seventy. Then I'll sit back and relax a little and enjoy what I've done over the years and what I have now. I'll see my kids and my grandchildren more often, for I've always worked a lot. I know family is very important, but if you're in business, that's your primary concern, and you have to be aware of that. Without a profitable business, your living can be tough. If you run a good business, you can be part of a good family and have religion in your life. I think that's all good.

I too enjoy being a partaker of this business. I'm a decent bowler. I average in the 220s, and I have gotten better over the years. Of course, lane conditions have gotten better, and good equipment has made it easier. I don't try to help people bowl unless they ask, but I have helped many over the years who have asked. We set aside time in the afternoon and turn on the lanes, and I let them practice. Then I give them a few tips to help improve their game. Sometimes by the year's end, they tell me they have raised their average five or ten pins, which is a good thing. I don't take credit for that. I feel that if people want to learn badly enough, they will take advice, practice, and improve. But I don't give advice if I'm not asked. Some people come just to have fun and fraternize with their friends, and I respect that.

I enjoy people. When I was young, I was much more involved, going to tournaments and doing basically anything pertaining to bowling. I attended bowling proprietor meetings and still do. I'm an officer in the Bowling Proprietors Association of America, and I was treasurer for a few years. We also held a health week benefit for some organizations. The proprietors put in money to help the Ronald McDonald House and the Albany Medical Center Miracle Network for children who were born weighing about two pounds. I went down to see them, and we all donated. These are some of the organizations I belong to and events I enjoy doing. Now I've moved to the country, and I'm beginning to enjoy my time alone. Being on the tractor, mowing the lawn without a cell phone, seems kind of nice too.

As a teen, I started working with a paper route. Then I worked for UPS, and finally I became the proprietor of the bowling center. Having my own money and independence was important to me.

I've reaped some of the benefits of hard work, which people have recognized over the years. I was voted into the Albany Men's Association hall of fame and the New York State Bowlers Proprietors hall of fame. A couple of years ago, I got the New York State Bowlers Proprietor of the Year award, which I thought was quite an honor. It was given by the Women's Bowling Association.

I'm fortunate to have a wife who doesn't mind if I say I'm coming home at six and then I come at ten. She puts up with this. Pat and I have been married thirty-five years. I incorporated three sons when I married her, and they have helped me out with the business over the years. As small boys, they worked here. My oldest, Wade, is still here. Greg worked here for a while and helped start our snack bar after renovating. Then he moved on to manage another restaurant. My youngest, Derrick, worked behind the machines. He has relocated and is now a successful lawyer. They made life good. I also have a daughter by my first wife, and she has two children. In all, I'm the proud grandfather of nine grandchildren.

Thinking about a change in my life, I almost sold the business a few years ago. I could have made a lot of money, and I probably would have been home doing nothing. But luckily, the deal fell through at the last minute, and now I breathe a sigh of relief, for I still enjoy working. Maybe in a few years my son will take over. A lot of people want to buy the center and turn it into something else. I always flirt with the idea, but then I think of the people in my life and what it would be like for them without it. We have families that have bowled here for years—and some for generations. The Benedetto and Ackert families come to mind. We love being an establishment that has received that kind of loyalty.

I can't imagine having all the money I need but having nowhere to go and no way to be a part of this! We can't go anyplace without running into someone we know. I say to my wife that I bet we'll see someone we know, and sooner or later, someone shows up. We went to California and ran into a pin boy who use to work here. Then we ran into people we knew in New York and Boston at baseball games. We went to Atlanta, Georgia, and had nothing to do, so we went to Six Flags. There we heard a woman say, "It's the man from the bowling alley!" It was Yolanda, one of our bowlers. She was there with her family and couldn't believe she was seeing someone she knew. In her excitement, she couldn't remember my name.

I feel bad that my past family can't see what I've done with the place. When I was sixteen, I told my grandfather that when I grew up I wanted to be just like him. He said, "No, you will never be like me and run the business like I do. Two years after I'm gone, the business will close." That was in 1976. And where are we now? It's 2014. Sorry, Gramps. We're still going, still working. It might look a little different now, but we're still here. Maybe his saying that has made me strive harder.

It feels good to have made so many friends over the years. I love the fruits of my labor, and I still get joy from providing a place where others can come and enjoy themselves.

George H. Hoffman

11

Denyse Cromwell-Mackey

IBM vice president of Global Technology Services, US Business Partner Channel

When I was young, I aspired to be a lawyer. I went to undergraduate school for law and got accepted into law school, but then I was blessed with a great opportunity to start working for IBM. When I was hired, I handled criminal justice accounts for the State of New York. I considered this to be close enough to what I had wanted to do. My father worked for IBM, and it had provided us with a good life, so I ended up going down the same path.

When I was in school, I never thought that what I was preparing for would enable me to do what I do now. I can truthfully say that the benefits I most appreciate from my education are knowing how to type, communicate, and lead people. These have been the skills I've carried forth to this day. I didn't go to law school, but I attended undergraduate and graduate school, and I got my master's degree with a concentration in law.

I truly love working for IBM. I love it on multiple levels. When referring to the point of my joy, my perspective changes.

When I first joined the company, my joy was that I worked for the company my father worked for, and that was it. It didn't matter what the company was; it was what my father did, so I liked it.

As time went on, I liked the company because I found I could be successful and make a lot of money. I was driven by financial goals.

Now I've come to see that I love the company for the skills I've developed as an individual. I would say that I've learned more from my experiences at IBM than I did in high school, college, or grad school. I have seen, in some cases, how our technology has saved peoples' lives—literally. This brings great reward to what I do.

Another element of joy at my job came from my employer's company values, which enabled me to embrace my desire to be a mom and to prioritize family without having to sacrifice my career. For me, joy is entwined between work and who I'm married to. The two are very tightly coupled and are critically dependent on each another.

I'm very blessed to have married the right person to be able to have a successful career. I have been able to work for a company that values family life and work life. It values women in the workforce and supports all their needs, enabling them to be successful in having both a career and a family. That's where I am right now.

My joy of employment has changed over time. When I first came to the company, they were moving from typewriters to personal computers. People thought that was exciting because they would be able to do everything faster. That's great, but it's not very meaningful. It doesn't make me feel like I'm contributing anything to society or life. I've been with the company for twenty four years as of July 2014. And in twenty-four years, I've seen our evolution to our current achievements and the kind of tasks I'm working on. This business is not about getting rid of a typewriter or buying a faster computer. Where everything used to be about becoming smarter and faster, it's now about changing how we live.

We have people working on simple things, like how to use smarter technology. For example, when you go to a hotel room, you don't stand at the shower with your hand under the water and wait for the water temperature to regulate before you get in. That drives up the hotel's operating costs. Hotels are now putting in smarter technology that will automatically know that you want the water to be a certain temperature and will regulate and set it accordingly.

Then you have a very different focus, where people are using computers to help find a future cure for cancer and to improve global education and the way our children learn.

To me, the notion of our becoming a smarter planet and smarter society is an amazing movement to see and be part of. This is going to be the future for our kids. The way we work and live today is nothing like it will be in the future. I'm seeing little pieces of that, from simple things—like regulating water temperature—to major things—like the "Watson" technology being used to figure out how to cure cancer. I love being part of that effort to change the world.

Madison, my ten-year-old, is picking up on all of it. One of her Mother's Day projects at school involved saying why she loved her mom. She said, "I love my mom because she works for a computer company, and when I grow up I want to develop my own computer, and it's going to be called The Peach 2.0.

I enjoyed the moment and said, "Your little sister and I will be right there with you." Meanwhile, little sister Makayla aspires to be the first female African-American president!

Madison had thought through all the details. She said, "Mom, we won't have to type. People don't type anymore. We all text with our thumbs rather than our fingers. I don't need to learn how to type." My words of wisdom encouraged her to learn how to type while she's in school, but she said, "Oh, no, we won't have to do that. The Peach 2.0 will be able to recognize your eyes. It's going to know who you are! You're going to be able to talk to it. There's not going to be anything like a keyboard. It will feel your fingertips and know what you want to do!"

I just said, "All right!" I get so much joy out of the influence I'm having on my children. Most important is seeing them both become strong and confident young girls.

I mentioned that IBM developed my skills to be a successful individual, and I have used those skills elsewhere. I would like to share two examples where I have nothing to say but "thank God."

The first was when my husband, Warren, became extremely ill. The doctors were going to discharge him from the hospital, alleging that an undiagnosed pulmonary embolism in his leg was nothing more than the result of a long flight to Aruba. If IBM hadn't taught me to be an aggressive salesperson—to respect authority and intellect but to always challenge and ask the right questions, to probe, to escalate and demand answers—I think I would have been a very docile person and would have just accepted what they said.

But because I *didn't,* because I leveraged technology and social media the way I'd learned to do at work, the outcome was a blessing. I got referrals through social networks of people in the state of Washington and found experts to see Warren and advise us on everything imaginable that could change the prognoses.

In the end, by leveraging technology, getting referrals, getting second and third opinions, and challenging the system, Warren ended up in CCU for a month with four life-critical situations. Had all my "work skills" not been fully deployed in a time of crisis, he would have been discharged. Surely God had his hand on the situation, and that saved my husband's life. In every aspect of work or personal life, the basic concept of "selling" applies to everything we do. Selling doesn't begin until somebody says no, questions no's, and really understand the root cause of issues.

The second example where work skills affected my personal life is in the financial arena. I have gotten so much joy from taking everything I've learned from work and applying it to church and actually seeing the tangible results. I love being a trustee and helping with the budget and seeing our new church edifice. I think God gives particular people to a church. Some have time, and some have skills, and both are not always present in one person. I haven't had time, but I've absolutely been able to use my skills there. Just seeing what that's done to help grow the kingdom of God is so rewarding. I would say to Warren, "I cannot believe the gratification I get out of this!"

You get joy in tidbits. It's an evolution. Your joy changes as you develop and share. Looking back and pulling others forward is another element of joy, as far as what I do in my job. I wish I had more time to do it more broadly because there are so many people in need—particularly women. I remember that I never intended to have children. I was going through a phase and was excited for financial success and was running after the corporate ladder. During that phase, children were not a thought in my head. Had I not met Warren, I probably would never have had children. After you have children, the person you are changes. You realize that life can't be about just you going forward. As a working mom, I evolved, changing who I am, how I operate, and how I work. Most importantly, I've changed the way I prioritize my time—whom I spend it with and what I do with it.

I strive to "look back and pull forward," meaning that I mentor others, particularly working moms. It's amazing how many times people say, "I don't know how you do it all." They say it casually, but they truly mean it. I think we all struggle with finding the right balance as mothers, wives, and career professionals. Any vote of confidence, any inspiration I can instill to "just do it" and "make it work," is rewarding. To see women strive for their achievements, aided by mentorship of other women, is something I've benefited from and enjoy giving back.

I love having those dialogues and being a role model for people. I love it that my children will never say that their mom is not around. Yet they know that I work really hard. I want them to see that and to grow up to be self-confident women who can aspire to be moms who can also continue to work.

I work a lot from home and from Delta Airlines seat 1A. I travel pretty much every week, but I keep it compressed so I can have my home time. I can't imagine it any other way. It's a great balance. The whole work-at-home situation is wonderful. I love it.

I think it makes me a better person and gives me a broader perspective. I want my children to constantly see the world. It's why we travel so much, and it's something I value.

I don't want this to be only about the joy of a career. I have described corporate joy because it is so intricately interlocked with the joy of having the right partner, which has allowed me to have the right career. I could never do what I'm doing if I didn't have the right partner. That is, in itself, a joy, and not everybody is fortunate enough to find that in life. It all has to work together.

Sometimes at the end of the day, I don't want to talk. My brain is challenged from thinking all day long. My job is not hard work; it's hard thinking—*very* hard thinking. But I like that. Putting every element and experience together, I aspire to do other things in life also. I look at this whole process as building blocks. As my joy transforms, my interest has transformed over time. I will eventually put all this together and completely turn the corner and head in a different direction.

My dad is eighty years old, and he worked for IBM for thirty-something years. If you want to talk about *joy*, you should know how he feels about his daughter being an executive at the company where he worked. He still likes to tell me how to handle things or asks about current company conditions. I smile and say, "All right, Dad."

As one of forty African-American female executives in the company globally, I feel accountable to represent the company well—not only to be more and do more, but to stand up and represent the values of the company in my personal identity and conduct.

There's a personal revelation that I try to live by: "Don't wait to need him to know him. Experience him." This came to my mind one night as I was driving home on a narrow, dark, curving road, which just so happens to be called Church Road. It was late, dark, and raining. I was coming home from the hospital after Warren had been admitted, and God spoke to me and said, "Aren't you glad you didn't have to need me to know me?" I felt such a sense of relief and gratification. To this day, I say that all the time. Everyone has a spiritual element, and I feel very free to represent who I am as a person, even in the workplace.

This statement not only applies to, first and foremost, a relationship with God, but it also applies to our relationships with other people. "Don't wait to need something to know someone—especially God." You have to network. You have to have a relationship and build a business around you. You have to "brand" yourself. Everything is sold because of a brand, including ourselves. Life is not all about working hard and delivering results. It's about how we conduct ourselves, how we're branded, and what's being said about us behind closed doors.

I always ask people, "What is *your* brand?"

12

Jasper McGill Sr.

Conrail-CSXT plant manager

During the past holiday season I had the opportunity to follow a long-standing southern tradition practiced by our family. We would go from house to house, spreading cheer and good will with family and friends.

As I was carrying out the tradition, I had time to visit a family who belonged to my church. During our fellowship, we talked about the question of joy.

I felt no hesitation in knowing or mentioning what my joy is. I am the youngest of nine children and the sole survivor of our family. My mother was a pastor and had her own church. My father was a deacon. My grandparents were faithful church members. We were familiar with the written Word and knew right from wrong.

I moved to Albany when I was eighteen, and let me say that I have lived my life to the fullest, doing whatever I wanted to, whenever I wanted to, and going wherever I wanted to go. Actually, I lived as though I would be around forever, as though everything would always be fun and games and good times. I did it all. I had the wine, the women, and the song.

I followed my parents' path and had a large family also. My role changed drastically as my children began to grow, for they all had their own different personalities, and I had to adjust in order to be effective in their lives. I was forced to become more involved and stable, even if I was reluctant to be the backbone and strong force in their lives, for I was still sowing my wild oats. It was quite a change for me.

The biggest reason for my changed lifestyle is this. Sometimes God has to give us obstacles to live through, experience, and overcome before we realize just what our lives are all about. Life definitely isn't all about self and our needs and desires. We are all here for a purpose. I was ruining my life and had to hit rock bottom before I made the change.

For quite a while, I had been staying out late, partying, and having what I called a good time, without proper nourishment and rest. I ended up in the hospital with many complications.

I have a rare blood type, and during my surgery they couldn't control the bleeding. Every transfusion went straight through my system. The hospital depleted all of my blood type available, and there was nothing left but clear fluid in my veins. My vital signs were barely visible, and the hospital staff thought I had passed away. They covered me with a white sheet but left the IV in my arm and wheeled me into the corridor to wait for family to arrive.

I don't know how long I was there, but I could hear the staff talking and saying that there was nothing else they could do for me. That was when I realized that I didn't want to die, and I began to earnestly— and I mean *earnestly*—pray and ask God to heal my body and change my life. I cried and prayed and began to sweat. Someone noticed that the sheet was wet, and when they uncovered me, my vital signs were readable. What a commotion followed that discovery!

It was like a miracle, for they had thought I'd passed away, but then I had vital signs again.

I knew that if I made it through this, I would try to live my changed life with the same passion and gusto I'd had before this experience. After my recovery, I tried to instill prayer and thanksgiving in my children.

My joy comes from knowing *who* I am and *whose* I am. I am blessed and converted and have had time to try to make amends for bad decisions made in the past.

If God can take a nothing like me and protect and keep me as he has throughout my life, he can do anything for anyone at any time. Oh, yes, sometimes we must go through rough valleys to know that we are not alone. We need those times to think about our lives and to examine the worldly things we think are vastly important. Our lives should be a testimony and witness of the God we serve.

I know I am protected. I planned to take five of my children on vacation. We packed our bags, loaded into my SUV, and were on our way. We were heading to North Carolina in anticipation of visiting relatives, seeing old friends, and relaxing. After driving for quite a while, we were tired, so I pulled over at a rest stop to take a nap before continuing. My son woke up and decided to take over the driving to allow us to make better time.

He set the cruise control on seventy miles per hour and soon fell asleep at the wheel. The swerving of the SUV woke me, and I realized what was happening. I called my son's name, reached for the steering wheel, and pulled it one way. He woke up and pulled it the opposite way, causing the vehicle to leave the road, go over an embankment, and flip eight times before finally resting on the roof.

We were all scared, fearful that this could be the end of our lives. The kids were screaming and crying, and all I could do was pray for their protection. I felt that if anyone should die, it should be me. After the carefree life I had lived, I deserved to die, but my children still had their lives ahead of them. When the SUV came to rest, my son got out and ran up the embankment to seek help. After being stunned for a minute, I realized that I needed to take immediate action.

I unfastened my seatbelt and assisted the others with theirs. I tried the doors and windows that would allow us to escape our imprisonment. There was complete chaos going on all around.

We were taken to the hospital and checked out. Yes, we were shaken up, bruised, and bleeding, and some of us had broken limbs, but all our lives were spared. God had answered my prayers. I again realized that only he could have kept us safe and brought us through an ordeal such as this.

Looking at the badly damaged vehicle, the broken glass, and the entire accident scene, anyone would surely believe that lives had been lost. But thankfully, God had given us another chance at life.

We were all blessed, and I am glad to be able to tell the story. I left the scene with an even greater awareness of my role in protecting family relationships and constantly supporting my children. I count this as just another one of life's lessons on my journey.

Many people say that I always have a smile on my face. I simply tell them that I have a lot to smile about.

I'm happy for the many friends I've made during my long tenure with CSXT. As I worked my way up to plant manager, I tried to remember that even as leaders, we are all only followers.

I'm thankful for all my Christian brothers and sisters. I've had the opportunity to worship and fellowship with them and really get to know them at my church over the years, and I have been enriched by the experiences.

I have gone through the ordeal of cancer, and I *thank God* that I am a survivor. Not only do I smile, but I sing. As the song says, "I sing because I'm happy.

I sing because I'm free, for His eye is on the Sparrow, and I know he watches me."

I count it all joy just to spread the good news of God's love, mercy, protection, and salvation. He loves me so, and there is nothing I can do but tell it!

13

Fouad A. Sattar, MD, FACOG, OB-GYN

Doctor, director, lecturer, and professor of clinical OB-GYN

It's amazing where my journey has taken me. It all started a long way from here.

I was born and raised in Cairo, Egypt. I earned my medical degree from Cairo University in 1966 and received my initial training in Cairo and Great Britain. Along with other duties, I ran a large fertility clinic at Guy's Hospital Medical School in London and the London Hospital Medical School, where I was working as a lecturer in OB-GYN, and where my interest in fertility medicine began. Then, in 1977 my wife and I moved to the United States.

After relocating, I joined the staff of St. Clare's Hospital in Schenectady, New York in 1979 as the director of the OB-GYN Educational Program for Family Practice Residents, and I also became a professor of clinical OB-GYN at Albany Medical College. I have a very active schedule, which includes assisting with the teaching and supervision of medical students and family practice residents. I try to teach my residents to be good physicians and healers, for that is our goal.

I always wanted to be a doctor, even when I was very young. When my playmates had scrapes and bruises, they always came to me for the cure. The more I learned as I got older, the more fascinated I became with the human body. I am really very grateful, absolutely grateful, that I love what I do and enjoy every minute of it. It never feels like a chore when I go to work. I feel like I'm going to see my friends, and that makes me happy.

Sometimes people say that patients unload their problems on doctors. When you have a problem, whom do you usually feel comfortable sharing it with? Sometimes it's easier to talk to your friends than to your close family because you feel more at ease. I enjoy that kind of interaction, and it's the reason I went into the OB-GYN field. It's one of the things I like about it.

The birth process is quite a journey, witnessed from beginning to end. Tests usually have to be performed to detect the existence of the fetus. At the beginning, it is so minute that it cannot be recognized. Then it becomes a bleep on the monitor, and then it grows and mysteriously becomes the little human life that comes out fully formed.

You talk about *joy*! Nothing gives me more joy than seeing the birth, the miracle. I am still fascinated after all these years. It is always one of the most beautiful moments I've experienced. It feels like God is handing the new life to me, and I have the privilege and exceeding joy to present his gift to the waiting mother. Those moments are special to me.

Many people ask about our waiting room, where the walls are covered with pictures of beautiful babies I've had the privilege to deliver. They also ask me how many babies I've delivered. I've never counted, and there are two reasons.

First, every one of them is special. I get so excited, it's as if each time is the very first time. I look at babies as individuals, not numbers.

And second, if I looked at them all and realized how many hours I worked, I would begin to feel tired. Then I might say, "Oh my God! Did I do all that?" It's a little like walking a long distance. You feel okay until someone tells you that you walked fifteen miles, and then your legs begin to ache. When you were caught up in the moment, nothing else mattered. You didn't feel the fatigue at all.

The truth is, it's a tremendous joy to share this beautiful experience with my patients and their families. Sharing this happy event with new mothers and their families is what drew me to obstetrics.

Another thing that gives me joy is this. I have very good patients who are appreciative and share their lives with me. What is more of a privilege than people sharing with me, their doctor, their most intimate feelings? They share, confide, and trust in me. That's a privilege that gives me happiness and joy. As many of them tell me, happiness is not in having money but in being content with what we have. I am very grateful and content with all these things in my life—not the material things but the inner feelings. These things cannot be measured, cannot be bought with money.

I am very much involved in teaching in the program at Ellis Hospital (which took over St. Clare's) and Albany Medical Center. When I see my students grow up, it's like they are my kids. As I see them become successful, it gives me a sense of pride and joy.

I've received a few awards. Recently I was nominated, via recommendations of other physicians, to join the academy of physicians of the Capital District Physicians' Health Plan (CDPHP). The newspaper talked about the many people I had mentored and all the care they provided for our community and our patients. I was so humbled and grateful because the chairman of CDPHP, who gave his time to come and introduce me, had been one of my students. He stood up and talked about my training him as a resident in 1981 and 1982. I am so proud to see his accomplishments and his success. That cannot be measured in material terms.

My joy is all of what I feel inside. I cannot hold it or touch it or measure it. The feedback from my students and patients is immeasurable. I believe that life is difficult enough as it is. We should not make it more difficult. Why not smile and be cheerful and help others as much as we can? When we are fulfilled inside, we are joyful. It's like praying in a church, synagogue, or temple and feeling comfort inside, which is a type of joy. When we sing with others, they are all brothers and sisters, not in business but in love for the Creator, and that is great.

I'm often asked if I delivered my own children. Actually, I didn't, but I was there, and I got to be the natural, nervous, worried father. It's not usually a good idea for physicians to deliver their own children. We are too close to the situation, too emotionally involved, and our emotions could cloud our judgment in making the proper decisions. It's too much to worry about, and if anything bad happened, we would never forgive ourselves.

I love to travel, and I recently went to London. Afterward, I joked with my friends that I hadn't wanted to say anything before I left, but I had gone to deliver the royal baby. I read that the young father Prince William mentioned he was worried and very excited during the delivery process. All new parents have those feelings; it's human nature.

I know about all these feelings, for I've been doing my job for a long time. Mostly there is joy, but there are other times when there is sadness. Even in the sadness, there is a time of joy, for then there is a time to comfort.

It makes me happy that I am able to help people in the most difficult times. I can comfort them by being at their sides and holding their hands, because all of us need support sometimes. That is a different kind of happiness. It's not that I am happy with the event itself but that I am able to help a friend in a difficult time. Those times have given me tremendous satisfaction because I was able to do something.

One of my heroes in medicine is an eighteenth-century obstetrician-gynecologist and one of the founders of Guy's Hospital Medical School in London, where I have taught. He said a lot of nice things that have touched me since the time I was a young student. One of his statements was about the patient: "Cure some, because you cannot cure all. Help more, because you can help more than you can cure. And comfort most—if not all, certainly the majority."

I have tried to follow his teaching and have gotten great satisfaction from comforting a number of my patients in difficult situations. I feel fulfillment when they rely on me, knowing that I am supporting them and standing by them. As I try to follow this motto, the delivering, the caring, the comforting, the helping, and the curing are what constitute my joy.

14

Valarie A. Scott

Principal of Howe Early Childhood Educational Center

How blessed I am to have a gift from God that gives me unspeakable joy! When I think about teaching, that's what comes to mind. It's a joy that runs through the threads of my life at all levels, both personally and professionally. I am certain that, of all the gifts I have from God, teaching is the one that gives me the most joy and puts a smile on my face.

I had an active family life even before I experienced school, but the moment I knew I was going to school, I was excited. Four weeks before school started, I had new clothes, pencils, crayons, and all the things I needed to begin the school year. From the time I started school at age four, I knew I loved school and wanted to be the *teacher.*

Even in kindergarten, I loved to play school, and I took home extra worksheets. I loved books and reading, and I set up my dolls like students in school. I can still remember giving my favorite stuffed bear a worksheet and crayon and telling him to do his best. Teaching was the most exciting job I could imagine.

I already had a Sunday school teacher I loved, and it was so much fun getting stars each Sunday. That wonderful teacher introduced me to new things about the Lord every Sunday, and another wonderful teacher introduced me to letters, sounds, and reading every day of the week in school. I was the happiest child you could imagine. By the end of that first year, the only role I played in my games was the teacher. If I couldn't be the teacher, I picked up my books and went home to play with my toys.

By third grade, I had written an essay that listed my personal goals, which my dad saved until shortly before his death. This series of goals had me ending up as president of the United States, but first I went through positions as a teacher, principal, and school board member. I was only eight, so I thought I had to be the governor and state senator before I could be president. Even then I believed that education was the road to achievement in life.

In fourth grade, I met a wonderful teacher, who would begin molding my joy, my love of teaching, by introducing me to peer tutoring. The first time I helped someone with a math assignment, I knew that I wanted to do this forever. I felt such excitement and fulfillment inside when the person got the right answer. I became consumed with reading and the way we learn.

My creative project in fifth grade was to learn how to make a collage and to understand how colors merge to make a piece of artwork. It then became my job to teach my small group how to create a finished product. We concluded by going outside and making a wall-sized piece of art on a sheet.

I wasn't upset to be the teacher's pet. I did not consider that a negative taunt. I loved clapping erasers, tutoring peers, and taking home extra books. I still have a *Dick and Jane* reader that one of the teachers gave me. I couldn't wait for after-school discussions with my teacher, and I often had my dad pick me up late so I could stay longer.

Over the years that followed, I realized that becoming a teacher was something that would be a part of my career. I was so certain of this that I began to seek out even more opportunities to be a group leader or teacher. I made my cousins line up at the bus stop and not eat their snacks as we prepared to go to camp. My cousin Lisa will readily tell everyone that I disciplined her when she was noncompliant about the rules for waiting for the bus. It was not my finest teaching moment, but you can ask her if she lined up and did not eat her snack from that moment on, or if our line stood close to the curb while waiting for the bus. We were one of the few stops without an adult, but we lined up well and were ready to board the bus when it arrived. My cousin said that was the moment when my family knew I was going to be a teacher.

I was in teaching mode as a senior in high school. In my AP English class, I made a frog game for kindergarten students as my senior project. Those cute little frogs jumped from lily pad to lily pad, and the game was based on Monopoly. Afterward, it became a gift to my little brother for him and his friends to play with. His fun began the day I took it home. It was no surprise to anyone that I knew my major from day one when I went to college. I chose Geneseo, a college known for education.

The joy I felt the first time I stood in front of a classroom over thirty years ago still makes me smile. In my mind, I can see the dress I was wearing. It was a blue floral print that hung just below my knees. I wrote "Miss Scott" on the board with chalk and introduced myself. I had the students write about what they had done over the summer.

It was a moment in time for me. Whether I taught small lessons or classroom lessons, it made no difference. I was happier planning lessons for students than I was going out with my friends. My friend Rich often tells about a holiday when everyone else was out at a picnic or at a lake. He had to call me and tell me to stop making ladybugs for number charts—and come out and have fun with my friends. I couldn't wait to see how excited my little kindergarten children would be to learn their numbers and see their ladybugs climb vines up to one hundred.

My first year out of college, there were no jobs, but I didn't give up. Whenever I got a chance to substitute, I was thrilled. The first summer, between subbing, I was given a chance to create my own summer school program. Five hundred dollars had been allotted to pay an aide and myself to run the program. This was the beginning of my leadership and supervision skills.

Since I was blessed to be able to live with my parents, my aide, Mary Jo, and I had a fun summer. We did art, cooked, and reviewed basic reading skills. I guess that was my lead into wanting to take teaching to the level of principal.

When I got the call to teach my own class, I didn't care that it started in December or that it had taken three years for me to get my own classroom. It was mine. Over the years, I have shared my joy of teaching with my family by allowing them to cut out, color, and bag projects for me. Even now, I get excited when I find something great to share with children—either in my Sunday school class or at school.

Over the first years of my professional career, there were moments when using what I feel is a God-given talent was the most special thing I could do. It was spiritually uplifting when I was able to expand my joy of teaching by taking on my own Sunday school class. It was awesome to be able to deliver the stories and pictures I had loved as a child. It was like having little Christian sponges, eagerly absorbing the material being taught.

When I received my first star as a child in Sunday school, it was as if someone had shone a light around the paper. I remember a picture of Jesus having a golden shine around it too. I felt a little of that same glow when I taught Sunday school for the first time. I realized then that, as much as teaching is the joy of my life, it was also giving me a *new* joy—for in good teaching, there is always good learning.

After twenty-five years of teaching, Sunday school still remains my personal fun moment of the week. As soon as I share information, and faces light up because they understand something I teach, I realize how much fun *I* had, learning the information that would give them a new skill. It's like a big rubber ball that keeps returning to me. When I learn new things to teach, life folds it back to me.

Even when my career took a turn and I left the classroom, I was still able to find joy in working with teachers and students at a different level. I enjoyed the privilege of hearing a school psychologist—one who had not worked with little children—tell me that I had taught her things, when actually I had learned so much about patience from her. It feels good to share career experiences with new teachers each year, to help them begin what has been the career journey of my life so far. It is so interesting to think that the joy I have in teaching will, in a few years, take a different turn. Who knows? This joy of education may, for a while, become the joy of learning.

Teaching has provided opportunities for some of the most awesome experiences of my life. When I was a younger teacher, I didn't have a lot of money for materials. I discovered an ad that said if I went to a workshop, I would receive nutrition materials for my classroom. I went to the workshop and subsequently became a volunteer.

As a result of volunteering, I had the chance to become an editor of national materials that were sent to classrooms. I taught the materials at workshops all across the country, became the chair of the New York state affiliate of the American Heart Association, and eventually became chair of a six-state region. In addition, I was able to volunteer all across the nation.

I've had other opportunities because of teaching. I provided a "Tips and Information" session for college students on how to get a job in education, and I've taught a class on leadership and workshops on diversity.

Ultimately, the joy in my life comes down to the words of a song we sing at church: the world didn't give me the thing that brings me joy, and the world can't take it away. When I experience something like delivering a personal quote to a national catalog or being on the alumni board of my alma mater, I know that these things have come about because of my love for teaching, which I have shared with so many over the years.

My joy in teaching comes through clearly. It's what I love, the thing that makes me smile. I can still see a particular child who struggled to learn something new. I can remember a student calling me after twenty years because he'd seen my name on something, asking if I was the teacher who had told him to get his life together because he had a responsibility as a young man to be a leader and make something of himself. He said my words had been a voice in the back of his head for twenty years. He had become a minister and wanted me to know that I had made a difference in his life.

I feel joy when I look at some of my former Sunday school students and hear them speak loudly as leaders for the Lord. There's a smile on my face when a former student introduces his or her child to me. This joy will stay with me, no matter where I go or whom I am with. What a blessing to have a joy that is God-given and God-driven!

What I think about joy is this: it makes the best days better, the good days great, and the worst days worth living.

Valerie A. Scott

15

David Soares

Albany County district attorney

I spent most of my childhood in Pawtucket, Rhode Island. My parents moved there when I was six years old, along with my four other siblings. I still enjoy returning to the area to spend leisure time with old friends and to reflect on our carefree days.

After high school, I received my bachelor's degree in communication from Cornell University. I believe in hard work, so I worked my way through Albany Law School as an intern for the Albany International Airport Authority and later for the Albany County, New York, district attorney's office. Upon graduation, I was hired as an assistant district attorney.

A large portion of my job consists of dealing with major crimes committed by citizens from our communities. We all have a role to play in the never-ending fight against crime. I strongly support and participate in youth programs, where community organizations and leaders try to blend education and jobs.

The question of what gives me joy threw me a curve. Most of us don't take time to consider what gives us joy. We are so focused on our electronic devices and our busy life schedules that we don't put much emphasis on our joy. It's one of the most perplexing questions that I have been asked in a long time. It forces me to think about the feeling of happiness. When do I feel it most?

I have most often felt happiness while in the service of someone else. When I am making others happy, I feel really good myself.

As I've gotten older, I love watching people do what they love. I enjoy watching television shows that pertain to cooking. The chefs are in the kitchen, mixing ingredients with passion and sharing with us how they create delicious meals. That is their field of expertise where they demonstrate their creativity. Musicians also show their love for what they do. They seem to be in another place when performing, and the joy they feel comes through on their instruments.

When we get older and more mature, we redefine what gives us joy. We experience joy in smaller things. Joy for me at the age of twenty might have involved a big, expensive car or other material items, but now there is no place for that in my life. Now I love giving presents and spoiling people in order to see and enjoy their reactions.

In my job, I get joy from trying to break the cycle of truancy and violence in our children's lives, first by ensuring and compelling school attendance. The range of crimes and defendants varies, but one constant remains: youths who abandon education are more likely to enter the criminal justice system than they are to graduate high school or attend college. I try to stay involved in the local school system.

My job gives me the opportunity to be the audible voice for the community, to help find solutions and implement change. Any new program or idea takes time. Most people are reluctant to make changes, so we must often proceed slowly. Each family must put first the proper upbringing of their children by staying involved in all their activities and knowing who their friends are.

Parental involvement is necessary to ensure the success of the child and to establish parental identity. I am involved in the School First task force to highlight awareness of the importance of education in the lives of our most vulnerable children. We want to encourage our youth. There are areas in our community where the youth are succeeding. The Albany Pop Warner Program involves a group of kids that come from some of the most challenging circumstances. They come together to play football and have been undefeated for years.

Many of these teams have gone to play in super bowls in New Jersey and other cities throughout the country. These young kids sometimes walk long distances to the practice field carrying their uniforms, helmets, and cleats. They are showing commitment. Football is a very difficult sport, but they come together and are mentored by their coaches. In the process, they grow and become successful.

But very few in this community know about the Pop Warner program. As a result, we are sponsoring a large pep rally to have fun, play games, and bring awareness to these deserving young athletes through the media. We have renamed the fan base "the Flock" and will provide T-shirts encouraging our community to come and join it. We are calling Bleecker Stadium "the Nest."

Projects like this really bring joy to our office. It's a result of the good things we try to do. We have to maximize the positive things we can do for our community. It's a struggle to find institutions in the heart of the community that keep people together.

When I was growing up, Sundays used to include church in the morning and various forms of outdoor activities in the afternoon. We cannot appeal to this generation with the same traditions. As a matter of fact, church needs to take place outside in order to get people to go inside. We do have a partnership with inner-city pastors to do the work needed to bring people in. Then we put our focus on caring, sharing, and respecting each other, along with worshipping our Creator. We all need this kind of structure.

Another thing that brings me joy is when I see kids doing well who have no reason to be doing well. They excel despite the fact that they have to work harder and deal with very difficult circumstances. This is nice to see. Here on the job, we don't focus on victories. Rather, we hope to see people struggle through their pain to get to another place, which is not always a perfect place but a better place than where they were. I take pride in much of what my coworkers do. They are not doing these things for me but for other people who come through this office. Helping people is my company's philosophy, and when it is implemented, it makes me feel good.

That's what we strive to do, and each of the sixty employees who work here gets to play a small roll. Some people leave here with their heads held a little higher and their loads a little lighter, having worked with us through very difficult experiences. They will remember us for the rest of their lives, and we will remember them for the rest of our lives. Sometimes people approach us in the community and thank us for the assistance and attention given to them by our staff under difficult circumstances. We can only feel good about this recognition of our positive involvement.

The public never sees what goes on after trials are concluded. That's when families gather, bond together, and share great relief. We get to be part of that. There are times when we are humbled by people. We think we have seen everything, and then the unexplainable happens.

Once a twelve-year-old girl sat in our office. A group of boys had been shooting a BB gun at her, trying to hit her in the head, and they'd shot out her eye. This young girl had absolutely no reason to be happy, but she played with my iPhone and sang songs, and at the end of the conversation, she said she didn't want us to ruin the lives of the kids responsible.

We all experience joy in our jobs when we witness firsthand the power of the human spirit and people's ability to love—even when they're in a personal space that should be filled with tension and anger. When we see the power of that level of forgiveness, it's humbling. And we see it quite often. We all learn and relate, though our lives touch on different levels.

There are many reasons I have a strong connection with kids. We have tried just about everything. I mean, I can't think of one activity we haven't done to help mentor our kids. Here are just a few examples.

- "Bring it to the court": the kids had to take classes in bike repair, video production, and computer building—all in order to earn playing time on the court
- Arts program for kids who enjoy step dance and other forms of performing arts
- Motocross: we partnered with Honda, which donated motor bikes, and kids had the opportunity to earn riding time

Everything is based on the merit system. Kids have to earn the rewards, which involve no expense to the kids. We provide shoes, sweatshirts, helmets, and all necessary equipment—plus a free meal.

This year we are focusing on school attendance. We have adopted six schools, with an emphasis on fifth graders. The staff and I teach a weekly program called Legalize. We take real cases and allow students to study the files, read the fact patterns, and then play all the roles in order to show them the consequences of choices they make.

We also encourage the students through achievement awards and T-shirts for attending classes for seven days. Kids can earn pizza parties if their class has the best attendance record for the week—and a large, outside party if their school beats other schools in attendance. These are all fun things that help motivate kids to stay in school and learn.

We must all do our parts to make a difference, and we always need good, dedicated adults to shepherd our kids. Our commitment and deep involvement is not political. I am thankful for the assistance and guidance I received when I was growing up. I experienced anger and rage, and I was confused by everything I went through at a very sensitive age. Yet there were people who put me on a different path. That same potential is present in every single child, even the ones growing up in the worst of circumstances.

It is unforgivable that we as an adult community allow these kids to throw away their lives at a very young age. The kids have to take some responsibility also, but when I look back at my own life, I see that even when I fell on my face, there was always someone who picked me up, dusted me off, and sent me on my way. Today there is a true *bottom* for kids, and there should never be a true bottom.

I will continue to raise awareness of the importance of education and parental and community involvement in our kids' lives, hoping that the final results will bring positive change. My joy and commitment lie in our youth, with emphasis on stopping crime before it begins. If people were geared toward the things that bring them joy, we would live in a much different and happier society.

16

Jacqueline S. L. Williams

Lobbyist and co-owner of State & Broadway Inc.

It is my joy to manifest the glory of God in my life so that I may live the best life I can. In doing so, I have learned to trust God. Trusting God means allowing him to intervene and guide me. This relationship defines who I am and charts the direction of my life.

Here are a few instances where I have let go and let God take charge, and he has surpassed my limitations.

On March 4, 1998, I requested a team meeting to announce to the firm that I would be leaving to become a competitor. This was my birthday gift to me. After the disbelief faded, the team was shocked once more when my friend and future business partner announced that if I was leaving, he was leaving with me.

That moment was empowering and priceless! I was the first nonlawyer lobbyist in this prestigious firm's history, and I was voluntarily saying good-bye after three short years. My decision had been in the making for generations.

I was destined to become an entrepreneur. My grandfather, who had no formal education, farmed his own land, which allowed him to care for his family. My mother, a self-starter, owns a successful health-care agency on Long Island, New York. When I was in high school, I wrote and signed her checks to pay the household bills, and I worked by her side as she launched her business. At the time, I never thought that I was in training to become the next generation of entrepreneurs. Today, I co-own a government relations firm that is widely recognized and highly successful.

To talk about my joy and not include my husband would be a severe injustice. Michael is a prayer asked and answered.

God exceeded my expectations when he gave me a husband. There is no other man more perfect for me. Before meeting Michael, I had less-than-notable dating relationships. Wanting more, I decided to pray for a husband. I had prayed for everything else, so why not a husband? My very specific prayer included a punch list of seven items: no preexisting kids, no drug use, a belief in God, no more than three years older than me, and so on. Those things, I thought, were paramount and absolute deal breakers if breached. Also, I told God I would not date until he sent me the man I was to marry.

I said my prayer in December 1991, and on February 15, 1992, I met the man who was to be my husband. It was a match made in heaven, but it needed a bit of work on earth. From the start, we were very attracted to one another, and we were inseparable. However, he was unequivocal: no marriage, and especially no children. As it turned out, God met half my list and gave someone else the other half, and he proved to me that love was greater than the rest. As they say, man plans and God laughs. That December, Michael proposed, and in April we were married.

More than twenty years later, our love grows deeper, stronger, and broader, and we keep Christ at the center of our marriage. Asking God to intervene in my life delivered me a loving husband, and God allows us to enjoy a wonderful marriage.

Years ago, my eldest son unexpectedly developed febrile seizures. He was six at the time. The slightest alteration in body temperature automatically triggered seizures. They increased in intensity, and we often had to remove him from school because of these episodes. As parents, we felt frightened and helpless. It was a very hard time for our family. He was medicated daily to gain control, but the medications were ineffective. Further, the doctor warned that he would soon be permanently labeled an epileptic. But God had his hand on our son—and a different plan for his future.

At that time, we attended church in Schenectady, New York. The church mother was blessed with spiritual gifts that she used to edify the church. It was not uncommon for her to deliver Spirit-derived messages to specific congregants. I was never one of those members who received a unique message. My family was fairly new to the church, and we'd had little or no connection with her, other than an occasional polite hello. Few people knew of our son's condition, and I am certain she was not among them.

As any good churchgoer knows, church mothers sit in the front pews. Oddly, one day she was sitting behind my family toward the very back of the church. From the start of the service, a voice in my head kept directing me to turn and touch her, but I refused. This mental banter kept up all through the service.

I barely paid attention to the preaching. When the service concluded, we rose to leave and hurry home for dinner.

Without warning, she asked me which of our children had a problem with his head. Stunned, I indicated my oldest child. Slowly she placed her hands on his head and said, "God said to tell you that he will not have a problem anymore." That was it! I will never forget it!

Walking away, I knew I had a decision to make that day. The question was clear: was I going to trust God with my son? My disobedience at church hung heavy on my heart. The Holy Spirit had been guiding me, and I had refused to listen. But God had a plan, and he earnestly wanted to execute it, so he had allowed the church mother to come to me. That was why I believe she was not in her customary seat that day.

I decided to let go and let God turn things around. My son stayed under medical care, but that day I discarded his medication. Never again did he experience another epileptic type of incident.

Unbeknownst to us at the time, the physician who was caring for our son was also molesting his male patients in the exam room. God was watching over my son. As parents, it was our rule to never leave our children unattended. This physician was arrested, convicted, and ultimately jailed. I wholeheartedly believe that our obedience turned our son's life in a different direction and protected him from harm.

Allowing God to order my steps has brought me boundless joy. I often reflect on and draw strength from my favorite poem, written by Marianne Williamson:

> Our deepest fear is not that we are inadequate. Our deepest fear is that we are powerful beyond measure. It is our light, not our darkness that most frightens us. We ask ourselves, Who am I to be brilliant, gorgeous, talented, fabulous? Actually, who are you not to be? You are a child of God. Your playing small does not serve the world. There is nothing enlightened about shrinking so that other people won't feel insecure around you. We are all meant to shine as children do. We were born to make manifest the glory of God that is within us. It's not just in some of us; it's in everyone. And as we let our own light shine, we unconsciously give other people permission to do the same. As we are liberated from our own fear, our presence automatically liberates others.

17

Wanda D. Yarbor

Contracting officer, NY Air National Guard

When I first learned I was being deployed to Afghanistan, I was angry and scared at the same time. But being in the military, I can't say that I was surprised, especially since I've been in for twenty years and have never had to deploy to a conflict.

I did a little research and learned that Afghanistan is squeezed between Russia, Pakistan, Iran, and China. It is almost seven thousand miles from the United States, and the regular flight duration from Washington, DC, to Kabul is fourteen hours, twenty-seven minutes. The population in 2013 was around thirty-one million. Pashto and Dari are the official languages, but many others are also spoken, and the country has been involved in conflict for years.

I had no idea what to expect. The thought of leaving my family behind was very unsettling. I would not have my husband there to talk to me, to share my day, to comfort me. I would not be able to play with my grandkids, to see their smiles, hear their laughter, and comfort their cries. The prospect was, to say the least, disheartening.

My send-off at the airport was very encouraging. When I got on the plane to leave Albany, I knew I was in for the experience of a lifetime. The trip took three days, with practically no sleep at all. By the time we got to a layover at a military installation, got checked in, followed all kinds of procedures, rules, and regulations, stood in line, ate, found a place to shower, dragged seven bags around, and got assigned a place to lay our heads down, it was time to go and wait for our next connection, which was not always guaranteed. It was one of the most frustrating times of my experience.

Arriving in Afghanistan, I was tired, hungry, and confused. I stood on the helipad until I could figure out where I was supposed to go. After finding my way to my assigned office, I quickly learned that I was expected to stay awake and immediately go into the office to work and get acclimated to the time change. So, being the good soldier I was, I did just that—after yet another frustrating experience obtaining a room assignment.

Although I had all kinds of preconceived ideas about my tour in Afghanistan, it was nothing like I expected. Yes, I was based in a country in the midst of conflict; yes, there were incidences of suicide bombers and fellow soldiers being killed every day; and yes, there were constant threats. But there was also a very human side to it.

Living conditions at the camp were different from home, but they were not the worst. I went there with the idea that we might be sleeping in tents or camping outside, but I was pleasantly surprised.

Some of us lived in container buildings, which were metal containers, joined together, that opened to the outside like motel rooms. A community bathroom in a separate container was about twenty feet from our doors. Others lived in container buildings that were stacked two or three high and were set up like dorms. The good thing about the stacked buildings was that the bathrooms were located inside. A few people were forced to sleep in tents, but that was usually a temporary situation.

Thinking I would bypass winter weather, I discovered, to my surprise, that the region I was stationed in had very similar temperatures and climate to where I lived in the United States. Sun and rain—and yes, even snow—found its way there. We saw nothing more than mountains, dirt, rocks, and very little greenery. I couldn't wait to get home and see trees, grass, and flowers.

Even though our surroundings appeared drab and dirty most of the time, the beauty was in the view of the mountains at sunrise and sunset—and when the snow settled on the mountain tops, affording the most beautiful caps imaginable. We take so much for granted.

The food was even more surprising. I would have expected to eat MREs (meals ready to eat), but we had decent hot meals and several different venues, including Burger King, Pizza Hut, and a Barbecue Hut.

Since I was there for the Thanksgiving and Christmas holiday seasons, I was able to partake in elaborate meals of beautifully dressed turkeys and hams, vibrantly carved fruit and vegetable displays, and extravagantly decorated cakes, pies, and cookies. Decorations more beautiful than anything I had seen at home were displayed effortlessly throughout the DFAC (dining facility). The feeling of joy, hope, and peace rang throughout the camp during the holiday season, and all was well.

A few of my colleagues and I even had the opportunity to indulge in a traditional meal with some of the local nationals that vend on camp. The food was prepared by them and their families and was absolutely delicious. They spread a huge scarf on the floor and displayed the food in the center, and then we all sat cross-legged on the floor around the food, in keeping with their tradition.

There were many volunteer opportunities to organize and distribute school supplies and clothing to local kids and to provide fuel sources for the community. Seeing the looks of gratitude and appreciation on their faces really warmed my heart.

During the few chances I had to leave camp and go into town, I saw nothing but poverty and despair. Everywhere I looked, there were rundown shacks and shops, kids in the middle of the road, peddling their wares, armed police, and military and security personnel.

But in the midst of all this, I found something that brought me joy: I was able to continue practicing my own faith with people who had the same values. My discovery that a gospel service was being held in camp on my first Sunday was music to my ears.

On Fridays, we worshipped in song and heard the Word preached. The choir, of which I was a member, sang with happy hearts every Friday and Sunday. Some of our services were even streamed live. Since we worked six days a week, twelve hours a day, and were always on call, having someplace to go and relax, unwind, cry, pray, or just vent was a saving grace for many there. My faith is one of the things that really kept me grounded and gave me peace before and throughout my deployment.

My joy comes from the gift of life, the freedom to worship, and the blessings we have in America.

Wanda D. Jaton

18

Reverend Dr. Damone P. Johnson, Honoree

**Preacher, teacher, musician, and
senior pastor of Metropolitan NTM
Baptist Church, Albany, New York**

My joy comes from the relationship I have with
God through the Lord Jesus Christ. There's a song
that says, "Jesus you're the center of my joy," and

that articulates the origin and service of my joy. We know that joy is a fruit of the Spirit, and the growth, development, and intensity of our fruit—expressed through joy—reflects our connection with Jesus Christ.

In other words, the closer I get to cultivating and developing my relationship with Christ, the sweeter my joy is. The relationship between my preaching and teaching ministries becomes a vehicle for sharing my joy. To give my joy away is what I'm really attempting to do. Whether it's in music, teaching, or community work, it's an interaction that becomes an avenue for giving my joy away.

When you do what God wants you to do, it gives you a sense of satisfaction, a sense of fulfillment and contentment. Someone has said, "Once I found what I was designed and purposed to do, I never worked another day in my life, because I would do this for free."

A former NBA player and frequent championship coach who really loves and enjoys the game was asked, "How do you know you love it?" He replied, "Because I would do it for free." Even now, he's trying to find a coach for his team's opposition, without getting paid for his effort. That's what gives him satisfaction and contentment.

Enjoyment comes from fulfilling my purpose. I began as a music major and political science major. At an early age, I had a call on my life to preach. I had been drawn to preaching and had focused on it more than a young person normally would. I told my mother—I think at age three or four—that I had to pastor and preach. She thought I was mixing my words, that I certainly must mean something else.

I loved music and started playing piano when I was five or six. Then I took lessons, studied in high school, and played for churches when I was fourteen. But I ran from the call to preach.

Subsequently, I went to Fisk University and was a double-major student, but I kept changing my major because I couldn't find contentment. I couldn't find my *purpose*. I was a political science major, a music major, and a public health major. My counselor said, "Damone, if you keep changing your major, it's going to take you ten years to graduate."

It was the summer of my junior year, and I felt that the counselor had hit on something. My situations was like going to a restaurant and seeing a menu with many appealing and appetizing items. I might get a side dish of this or a side of that, but the main entrée was what I wanted most. A lot of things looked good, but I had to order what I wanted most. I asked myself,

"What do you feel that God is *most* telling you to do?" And my answer was, "To preach his Word."

In my junior year, I changed my major yet again to religion and philosophy. The schedule required twenty-four credits. I finished in two years, and then I preached my initial sermon in the fall of 1995.

I grew up in church under awesome pastors. My childhood pastor was phenomenal, and I called him "master pastor." Dr. Andrew J. Brown of St. John Baptist Church in Indianapolis, Indiana, was twenty-three when the church called him, and he served for forty-four years. Dr. Thomas L. Brown, my current pastor, is also impactful and effective. I have had other mentors, teachers, and coaches who have aided in my development and still do.

I was very close to the church. My mother worked as the administrative assistant to the pastor when I was young. That was where she worked and where we worshipped. I spent a lot of time around the church and the pastor. He and the first lady felt like grandparents to me. They were great people who loved God's people and loved working in the church and community. That was their joy, which they conveyed to me. My mother is very proud that I surrendered to the call of God.

I initially ran from the call to preach because I saw some of the things my pastor went through. As a result of being really close to him, I was able to see what the general public couldn't. I saw the impact of his position, and I didn't know if I wanted to commit to facing all of that. I looked at my own abilities and wondered if I had what it took to pull off what God wanted me to do.

Now, as a pastor, I get very excited when people join our congregation after the invitation has been extended. The Bible says, "Heaven rejoices when one comes," so certainly, when ten or fifteen come, it's exciting. Those people are now availing themselves of the experience of joy. We are thankful for the growth of our church. As it says in Acts, "The Lord added to the church as he saw fit." At the end of the day, it's the Lord who brings about the growth.

We attempt to be one church that ministers to multiple generations. I'm very intentional in that. Whether through music, ministries, Christian education, preaching, or teaching, we try to appeal to all ages. We have different ministries for people in different stages of life, whether they're married, single, young adult, senior saints, children, or youth. This has been a need in our area, and our outreach has attracted many to come.

Church growth and outreach were something I experienced early on, for I grew up in an extremely large church under Dr. Andrew J. Brown. Through outreach, the pastor was very involved in politics and community, as well as things within the church. He was able to communicate well on both sides. He had about thirteen or fourteen hundred members who came to church on Sundays, and he had a huge radio and TV ministry. This was before African-American churches, particularly in that area, were doing so. He was sort of a pioneer and trailblazer in the church and in spreading the Word beyond the four walls of the church. It was nothing to see fifteen or twenty people join the church on a Sunday. He had an extremely magnetic personality as a preacher, singer, pastor, and great ministry leader.

There was always a program or some kind of a movement at the church, which was extremely appealing. Just being there affected my development. I wasn't really paying attention, but without knowing it, I was being influenced by that environment. Being around the staff, I was gaining experience, for they were very busy and involved in giving away clothing and supporting the needy in the community.

The mayor came every year, and the governor also stopped by, for Dr. Brown was very engaged in the social and political aspects of the community. As a matter of fact, every year there's a gathering called the Indiana Black Expo. At its height, as many as four or five hundred thousand people came. We were very involved in that. Actually, it was the brainchild of

Dr. Andrew J. Brown. Live concerts drew many stars, entertainers, and athletes for the summer celebration, which is ongoing. It doesn't have the appeal it once had, but it was once nothing to see top entertainers, actors, and singers of the time as we walked through the convention center. It was a culture of development.

My mother worked very closely with the Black Expo as the liaison for the church and later with the director of the event, Rev. Charles Williams, who was also an associate minister of the church.

My own ministry certainly reflects all these influences. I am concerned about serving people through our community day activities, Thanksgiving giveaways, development of staff, ministries, and facilities, and helping in youth and senior ministries.

Metropolitan has been blessed with such tremendous pastoral leadership; it's historical. Dr. Earnest E. Drake was phenomenal and visionary in building not only the church but also the senior housing across the street. I followed in the pattern of Pastor Rexford P. Charlow and, of course, the founding pastor, Dr. John B. Holmes. They established the church as a very biblically based entity that was strongly rooted in biblical principles. The outgrowth of their ministries extended to building churches, community ministry, the housing across the street, radio, television, and so on.

As Dr. Clifford Jones said, "Pastors don't make churches. Churches make pastors." A church can have a great leader, but, as John Maxwell said, "If you're leading and no one is following, you're just taking a walk!" Pastors need people who are willing to follow leadership, and they trust that people will follow them as they follow Christ. It's a blessing to be at such a church, for not all churches are like that.

I also believe that a preaching moment is at its best when the fruit of our labor is expressed in changed lives. There are those who claim that their lives, and the lives of their families, have been changed dramatically. That's an extension of joy, a result of really sharing and giving away my joy. To see the impact is special. I believe the Bible is powerful enough to transform, change, lead, and guide. When the Lord leads me to direct or guide the church in a particular direction, or to shift or correct some things, it's always based on the Word of God. That's the source. Our book of faith and practice has to be the Bible.

Everyone has an opinion, but when it comes to the Word of God, it takes priority. Whatever the Word says goes. Our opinions and thoughts can fluctuate, but the Word is consistent. That's why everything is based on God's Word. Whether it's community work, social work, television, radio, Facebook, the Internet, or a website, it's all still based on the Word of God, which is the foundation of everything else. And that's another aspect of joy: its cultivation.

In Philippians 1, when Paul was in a Roman prison, people thought his preaching and teaching had ended. There were many who attacked him and his ministry, but he said, "This has come for the furtherance of the gospel." In other words, what he was going through was furthering God's message. This is a picture of the special agents of an army who cut the trees and prepare the way for the entire army to go through. Paul's imprisonment was clearing the way so the Word could go through. To have that perspective—to know that all our challenges and difficulties happen so that the testimony of the gospel might go through—is a joy.

Later, Paul said, "Rejoice in the Lord always; —and again I say, rejoice." (Philippians 4:4) The outgrowth of joy is not just the enjoyment of what we do but the ability to *rejoice* through problems, hurts, and challenges. It's easy to express joy in good times on the mountaintop, but it's those difficult valley experiences that try us. Joy is really an outgrowth of the fruit of the Spirit, so regardless of what's going on around me, I can still have joy. It's not predicated on my rapport with people. Think about David and Saul in the Bible. Despite David's difficulties, he still had a sense of joy because it was not based on what Saul or anyone else did to him. It was based on his fellowship and communion with God.

So, what do we do with our joy? We know that the Sea of Galilee has an inlet where water comes in, and there's an outlet to let the water out. It's in a fertile area, and the vegetation around it is rich and refreshing. But the Sea of Galilee flows into what is called the Dead Sea. It's called the Dead Sea because what flows in has no way out, and everything around it is dead. It always receives, but it never gives out. When you are able to *share* and *give your joy away,* that makes your life real and refreshing, and it opens you up to receive even more.

19

Ultimate Joy

—Margaret T. Coleman

I will close this book with one last entry.

Can you imagine Jesus finding joy in doing his Father's will in order to save us? He had to give up his Father's presence and leave his heavenly home, a place of peace, love, and happiness. He was born into the human race in a humble stable, grew up in a small town, lived modestly, and was misunderstood, lied about, talked about, beaten, and eventually killed in one of the most painful forms of death: crucifixion. He endured all of this for us because of our sins, faults, bad decisions, lies, and disobedience.

Jesus didn't do anything wrong. He didn't deserve the treatment he received, but he endured it just for us. What love this is!

Jesus loves us, but he knew he would be returning to his Father in heaven, and he didn't want us to be alone. So he left a comforter, the Holy Spirit.

All this he did for his special creation—you!

He knew that all he went through was temporary, that at the end of his time on earth, he would be reunited with his Father in heaven forever. Oh, what a day that was! What joy, unspeakable joy, it was!

Because of what Jesus did for us—for lost sinners— we can come back to fellowship with our heavenly Father. Jesus was joyful because his mission was completed, and he returned to his rightful place at the right hand of his Father. Out of his pain came *joy*!

20

Closing Comments

We all have a story to tell, and I think you are cheating yourself if you don't find the one thing that makes your heart sing and makes your life complete. All contributors to this book have shared their joy, and it was a pleasure to have their participation.

Hopefully, these stories will light a fire within you that will continue to burn until you find your own joy.

I am grateful for the opportunity to present these demonstrations of personal, loving joy.

As nature changes with each new season, there is something to strive for and commit to: finding your joy.

Search for it.

Find it.

And, by all means, enjoy it!

About the Author

Margaret T. Coleman is formerly a native of a small town near Woodstock, New York. Presently, she is a local resident of the beautiful upstate New York region. She is an avid bowler, faithful church member, volunteer to local charities, and enjoys traveling and reading. She graduated from Albany High School and Comptometer Business School.

She gained experiences from employment at National Commercial Bank (Key Bank) in the accounting department, General Motors Acceptance Corporation, and seasonal duties with the Department of Taxation and Finance.

She has spent countless hours sharing financial freedom information and serving as a facilitator in the new member orientation ministry at church.

She is married and is also the mother of two children.